# FILIGREE
## collection three

to my friend

Peter Christian Christensen

# CONTENTS

# FILIGREE

... is simply a celebration of crochet.

Using Rowan's new 'Summerlite' cotton yarn, this beautiful and very feminine collection of 10 openwork designs reflects the true elegance of this traditional craft. Some of the designs are a combination of crochet and knit, each complimenting the other creating a sophisticated and contemporary look. The colours I've used are the quintessential summer colours of white and pale grey, which show the authentic beauty of the crochet stitches. I hope you enjoy making these garments as much as I enjoyed designing them.

Happy crocheting!

Marie X

Hollyhock

Lupin

Lupin

Aster

Aster

Daisy

Daisy

Buttercup

Anemone

Peony

Peony

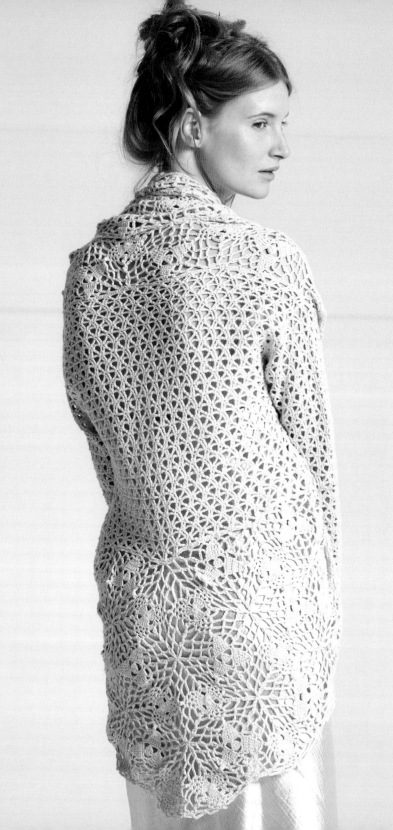

Rose

Rose

Carnation

Tulip

Tulip

Photography: Peter Christian Christensen
Styling & Art Direction: Marie Wallin
Hair & Make-Up: Frances Prescott
Model: Georgia Waters

# GALLERY

**HOLLYHOCK**
Main image pages 6, 8 & 9
Pattern page 64

**LUPIN**
Main image pages 10, 11 & 13
Pattern page 55

**ASTER**
Main image pages 14, 15 & 16
Pattern page 46

**DAISY**
Main image pages 18, 19 & 20
Pattern page 66

**BUTTERCUP**
Main image pages 22 & 23
Pattern page 58

**ANEMONE**
Main image pages 24 & 25
Pattern page 48

**PEONY**
Main image pages 26, 27, 28 & 29
Pattern page 51

**ROSE**
Main image pages 5, 30, 31 & 33
Pattern page 42

**CARNATION**
Main image pages 34, 35 & 41
Pattern page 60

**TULIP**
Main image pages 36, 37 & 38
Pattern page 44

PATTERNS

# R O S E

|  | S-M | L-XL | XXL |  |
|---|---|---|---|---|
| To fit bust | 81-86 | 91-107 | 112-127 | cm |
|  | 32-34 | 36-42 | 44-50 | in |

**Rowan Summerlite**

|  | 7 | 9 | 11 | x 50gm |
|---|---|---|---|---|

(photographed in Pure White 417)

**Crochet hook**
2.50mm (no 12) (US B1/C2) crochet hook

**Tension**
Each motif measures 8 cm square using 2.50mm (US B1/C2) crochet hook.

**Crochet abbreviations**
ch = chain; dc = double crochet; sp(s) = space(s); ss = slip stitch; tr = treble; yoh = yarn over hook; tr2tog = (yoh and insert hook as indicated, yoh and draw loop through, yoh and draw through 2 loops) twice, yoh and draw through all 3 loops on hook; tr3tog = (yoh and insert hook as indicated, yoh and draw loop through, yoh and draw through 2 loops) 3 times, yoh and draw through all 4 loops on hook.

BASIC MOTIF
Using 2.50mm (US B1/C2) crochet hook make 4 ch and join with a ss to

form a ring.
**Round 1 (RS):** 3 ch (counts as 1 tr), 2 tr into ring, (5 ch, 3 tr into ring) 3 times, 5 ch, ss to top of 3 ch at beg of round.
**Round 2:** 3 ch (does NOT count as st), miss st at base of 3 ch, tr2tog over next 2 tr, *5 ch, 5 tr into next ch sp**, 5 ch, tr3tog over next 3 tr; rep from * to end, ending last rep at **, 2 ch, 1 tr into top of tr2tog at beg of round.
**Round 3:** 1 ch (does NOT count as st), 1 dc into ch sp partly formed by tr at end of last round, *5 ch, 1 dc into next ch sp, 5 ch, tr3tog over first 3 tr of next group of 5 tr; 3 ch, tr3tog over last 3 tr of same 5 tr group (centre tr of this group of 5 tr is used for **both** tr3togs)**, 5 ch, 1 dc into next ch sp; rep from * to end, ending last rep at **, 2 ch, 1 tr into dc at beg of round.
**Round 4:** 1 ch (does NOT count as st), 1 dc into ch sp partly formed by tr at end of last round, *7 ch, 1 dc into next ch sp, 9 ch, ss to top of dc just worked, 7 ch, 1 dc into next ch sp, 3 ch, 1 dc into next ch sp, 5 ch, ss to top of dc just worked, 3 ch, 1 dc into next ch sp; rep from * to end, replacing dc at end of last rep with ss to first dc.
Fasten off.
Basic motif is a square. In each corner, there is a loop of 9 ch and at centre of each side there is a loop of 5 ch. Between centre loop and corner loop there are a further 2 ch sps – one of 3 ch and one of 7 ch. Join motifs when working round 4 by replacing the centre "1 ch" of the corner and centre loops and the 7-ch sp with "1 ss into corresponding ch loop or sp of adjacent motif". (**Note:** Motifs are NOT attached along the shorter 3-ch sp, so they are attached at each corner and 3 points along each side.)

SWEATER
Following appropriate diagram, make and join 140 [164: 216] basic motifs to form shape shown in diagram. Join all motifs so that RS is uppermost **except** those marked with * - these should be joined so that **WS** is

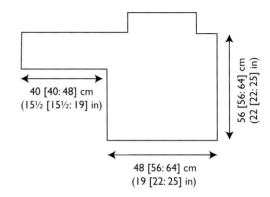

40 [40: 48] cm
(15½ [15½: 19] in)

56 [56: 64] cm
(22 [22: 25] in)

48 [56: 64] cm
(19 [22: 25] in)

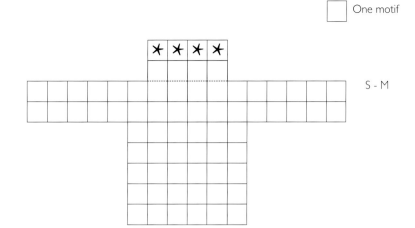

S - M

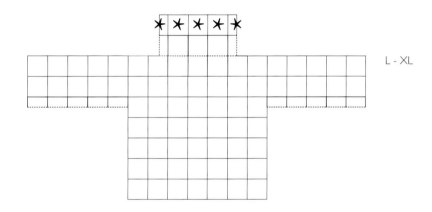

L - XL

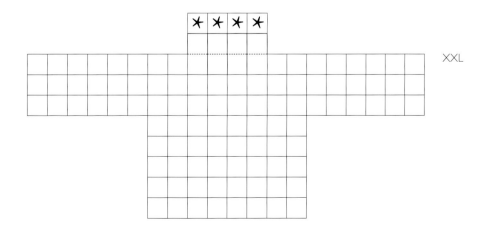

XXL

One motif

uppermost (for collar turn-back). Diagram shows front of garment – back is identical and both sections are joined, leaving cuff, hem and collar neck edges open. On size L-XL, half motifs on diagram indicate a motif folded in half and joined to both front and back. (The folded edge is indicated by the dashed line.) Dotted line on diagram indicates neck opening line.

MAKING UP
Press as described on the information page.
Fold last band of motifs to RS around top of collar section to form collar turn-back.
See information page for finishing instructions.

# T U L I P ●●

|  | S | M | L | XL | XXL |  |
|---|---|---|---|---|---|---|
| To fit bust | 81-86 | 91-97 | 102-107 | 112-117 | 122-127 | cm |
|  | 32-34 | 36-38 | 40-42 | 44-46 | 48-50 | in |

**Rowan Summerlite**

|  | 7 | 8 | 9 | 10 | 12 | x 50gm |
|---|---|---|---|---|---|---|

(photographed in Pure White 417)

## Needles
1 pair 2¼mm (no 13) (US 1) needles
1 pair 2¾mm (no 12) (US 2) needles
Cable needle
2.50mm (no 12) (US B1/C2) crochet hook

### Tension
37 sts and 37 rows to 10 cm measured over patt using 2¾mm (US 2) needles.

### Special abbreviations
**C6B** = slip next 3 sts onto cable needle and leave at back of work, K3, then K3 from cable needle; **C6F** = slip next 3 sts onto cable needle and leave at front of work, K3, then K3 from cable needle.

### Crochet abbreviations
**ch** = chain; **dc** = double crochet.

### BACK
**Lower section**
Using 2.50mm (US B1/C2) crochet hook make 139 [149: 173: 183: 207] ch.
**Row 1 (RS):** 1 dc into 2nd ch from hook, 1 dc into each ch to end, turn. 138 [148: 172: 182: 206] sts.
**Row 2:** 1 ch (does NOT count as st), 1 dc into each dc to end, turn.
Rep last row 8 times more, ending with RS facing for next row.
Now work strips as folls:

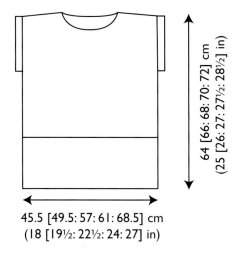

64 [66: 68: 70: 72] cm
(25 [26: 27: 27½: 28½] in)

45.5 [49.5: 57: 61: 68.5] cm
(18 [19½: 22½: 24: 27] in)

**Row 11 (RS):** 1 ch (does NOT count as st), 1 dc into first dc, *make 50 [53: 56: 62: 65] ch, now work back along this length of ch as folls: 1 dc into 2nd ch from hook, 1 dc into each ch to end**, now work into top of row 10 as folls: 1 dc into each of next 2 dc; rep from * to end, ending last rep at **, now work into top of row 10 as folls: 1 dc into last dc.
69 [74: 86: 91: 103] ch strips.
Fasten off.
Taking great care not to twist strips and to work across strips in correct order, now join strips at upper edge as folls:
**Row 12 (WS):** Attach yarn to tip of last strip, 1 ch (does NOT count as st), 1 dc into tip of last strip, *1 ch, 1 dc into tip of next strip; rep from * to end, working 2 dc into tip of end strip, turn.
138 [148: 172: 182: 206] sts.
**Row 13:** 1 ch (does NOT count as st), 1 dc into each of first 2 dc, *1 dc into next ch space, 1 dc into next dc; rep from * to end, turn.
**Rows 14 to 23:** As row 2.
Fasten off. (Lower section should meas approx 24 [25: 26: 28: 29] cm.)

## Upper section
With RS facing and using 2¾mm (US 2) needles pick up and knit 138 [148: 172: 182: 206] sts from top of last crocheted row of lower section – this is one knitted st for each crocheted st.
**Next row (WS):** P8 [5: 9: 6: 10], inc purlwise in next st, (P3, inc purlwise in next st) 30 [34: 38: 42: 46] times, P9 [6: 10: 7: 11].
169 [183: 211: 225: 253] sts.
Now work in patt as folls:
**Row 1 (RS):** K1, *sl 1, K1, psso, yfwd, C6B, K6; rep from * to end.
**Row 2 and every foll alt row:** K1, *P2tog, yrn, P11, K1; rep from * to end.
**Row 3:** K1, *sl 1, K1, psso, yfwd, K12, rep from * to end.
**Row 5:** K1, *sl 1, K1, psso, yfwd, K3, C6F, K3, rep from * to end.
**Row 7:** As row 3.
**Row 8:** As row 2.
These 8 rows form patt.
Cont in patt until upper section meas 36 [37: 38: 38: 39] cm **from pick-up row**, ending with RS facing for next row.

## Shape shoulders
Keeping patt correct, cast off 5 [6: 7: 8: 10] sts at beg of next 6 [6: 2: 4: 6] rows, and - [-: -: 8: 9: -] sts at beg of foll – [-: 4: 2: -] rows. 1
39 [147: 165: 175: 193] sts.

## Shape back neck
**Next row (RS):** Cast off 5 [6: 8: 9: 10] sts, patt until there are 30 [33: 38: 42: 48] sts on right needle and turn, leaving rem sts on a holder.
Work each side of neck separately.
Dec 1 st at neck edge of next 6 rows **and at same time** cast off 6 [6: 8: 9: 10] sts at beg of 2nd and foll 2 [0: 2: 2: 1] alt rows, then – [7: -: -: 11] sts at beg of foll – [2: -: -: 1] alt rows.
Work 1 row.
Cast off rem 6 [7: 8: 9: 11] sts.
With RS facing, slip centre 69 [69: 73: 73: 77] sts onto a holder, rejoin yarn and patt to end.
Complete to match first side, reversing shapings.

FRONT
Work as given for back until 8 [8: 12: 12: 16] rows less have been worked than on upper section of back to beg of shoulder shaping, ending with RS facing for next row.

## Shape front neck
**Next row (RS):** Patt 57 [64: 78: 85: 99] sts and turn, leaving rem sts on a holder.
Work each side of neck separately.
Keeping patt correct, dec 1 st at neck edge of next 7 [7: 10: 10: 10] rows, then on foll 0 [0: 0: 0: 2] alt rows. 50 [57: 68: 75: 87] sts.
Work 0 [0: 1: 1: 1] row, ending with RS facing for next row.

## Shape shoulder
Cast off 5 [6: 7: 8: 10] sts at beg of next and foll 3 [4: 0: 1: 5] alt rows, then 6 [7: 8: 9: 11] sts at beg of foll 3 [2: 6: 5: 1] alt rows **and at same time** dec 1 st at neck edge of next 3 [3: 1: 1: 1] rows, then on foll 3 [3: 4: 4: 4] alt rows.
Work 1 row.
Cast off rem 6 [7: 8: 9: 11] sts.
With RS facing, slip centre 55 sts onto a holder, rejoin yarn and patt to end.
Complete to match first side, reversing shapings.

MAKING UP
Press as described on the information page.
Join right shoulder seam using back stitch, or mattress stitch if preferred.

## Neckband
With RS facing and using 2¼mm (US 1) needles, pick up and knit 22 [22: 26: 26: 30] sts down left side of front neck, K across 55 sts on front holder as folls: (K2, K2tog, K1) 11 times, pick up and knit 22 [22: 26: 26: 30] sts up right side of front neck, and 8 sts down right side of back neck, K across 69 [69: 73: 73: 77] sts on back holder as folls: K4 [4: 1: 1: 3], (K2, K2tog, K1) 12 [12: 14: 14: 14] times, K5 [5: 2: 2: 4], then pick up and knit 8 sts up left side of back neck. 161 [161: 171: 171: 183] sts.
**Row 1 (WS):** P1, *K1, P1, rep from * to end.
**Row 2:** K1, *P1, K1, rep from * to end.
These 2 rows form rib.
Cont in rib for a further 3 rows, ending with RS facing for next row.
Cast off in rib.
Join left shoulder and neckband seam. Mark points along side seam edges of back and front 18 [19: 20: 21: 22] cm either side of shoulder seams (to denote base of armhole openings).

## Armhole borders (both alike)
With RS facing and using 2¼mm (US 1) needles, pick up and knit 111 [117: 123: 129: 135] sts evenly along armhole opening edges between marked points.
Beg with row 1, work in rib as given for neckband for 5 rows, ending with RS facing for next row.
Cast off in rib.
See information page for finishing instructions.

ch, *8 ch, miss 8 ch, 1 tr into each of next 8 ch; rep from * to last ch, 1 tr into last ch, turn. 8½ [10½: 12½] patt reps.

Now work in patt as folls:

**Row 1**: 3 ch (counts as first tr), miss tr at base of 3 ch, *1 tr into each of next 3 tr, 2 ch, miss 2 tr, 1 tr into each of next 3 tr**, 8 ch, miss 8 ch; rep from * to end, ending last rep at **, 1 tr into top of 3 ch at beg of previous row, turn.

**Row 2**: 3 ch (counts as first tr), miss tr at base of 3 ch, *1 tr into each of next 3 tr, 2 ch, miss 2 ch, 1 tr into each of next 3 tr**, 3 ch, 1 dc into next ch sp 2 rows below enclosing ch sp of previous row in this st, 3 ch; rep from * to end, ending last rep at **, 1 tr into top of 3 ch at beg of previous row, turn.

**Row 3**: 3 ch (counts as first tr), miss tr at base of 3 ch, *1 tr into each of next 3 tr, 2 tr into next ch sp, 1 tr into each of next 3 tr**, 8 ch, miss (3 ch, 1 dc and 3 ch); rep from * to end, ending last rep at **, 1 tr into top of 3 ch at beg of previous row, turn.

**Row 4**: 11 ch (counts as 1 tr and 8 ch), miss tr at base of 11 ch and next 8 tr, *1 tr into each of next 8 ch, 8 ch, miss 8 tr; rep from * to last st, 1 tr into top of 3 ch at beg of previous row, turn.

**Row 5**: 11 ch (counts as 1 tr and 8 ch), miss tr at base of 11 ch and next ch sp, *1 tr into each of next 3 tr, 2 ch, miss 2 tr, 1 tr into each of next 3 tr,

# A S T E R ●●

| | S-M | L-XL | XXL | |
|---|---|---|---|---|
| To fit bust | 81-86 | 91-107 | 112-127 | cm |
| | 32-34 | 36-42 | 44-50 | in |

**Rowan Summerlite**

| | 5 | 7 | 9 | × 50gm |
|---|---|---|---|---|

(photographed in Washed Linen 418)

## Crochet hook

2.50mm (no 12) (US B1/C2) crochet hook.

## Tension

2 st patt repeats (32 sts) to 11 cm and 2 row patt repeats (16 rows) to 14 cm using 2.50mm (US B1/C2) crochet hook.

## Crochet abbreviations

**ch** = chain; **dc** = double crochet; **dtr** = double treble; **sp(s)** = space(s); **ss** = slip stitch; **tr** = treble; **ttr** = triple treble; **yoh** = yarn over hook; **dtr3tog** = *(yoh) twice and insert hook as indicated, yoh and draw loop through, (yoh and draw through 2 loops) twice, rep from * twice more, yoh and draw through all 4 loops on hook.

## BACK and FRONT (both alike)

Using 2.50mm (US B1/C2) crochet hook make 140 [172: 204] ch.

**Foundation row (RS):** 1 tr into 4th ch from hook, 1 tr into each of next 7

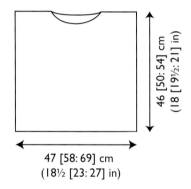

46 [50: 54] cm
(18 [19½: 21] in)

47 [58: 69] cm
(18½ [23: 27] in)

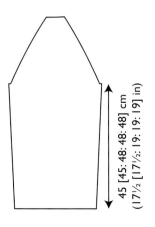

45 [45: 48: 48] cm
(17½ [17½: 19: 19] in)

8 ch, miss next ch sp; rep from * to last st, I tr into 3rd of I I ch at beg of previous row, turn.

**Row 6**: 6 ch (counts as I tr and 3 ch), miss tr at base of 6 ch, *I dc into next ch sp 2 rows below enclosing ch sp of previous row in this st, 3 ch**, I tr into each of next 3 tr, 2 ch, miss 2 ch, I tr into each of next 3 tr, 3 ch; rep from * to end, ending last rep at **, I tr into 3rd of I I ch at beg of previous row, turn.

**Row 7**: I I ch (counts as I tr and 8 ch), miss (tr at base of I I ch, 3 ch, I dc and 3 ch), *I tr into each of next 3 tr, 2 tr into next ch sp, I tr into each of next 3 tr, 8 ch, miss (3 ch, I dc and 3 ch); rep from * to last st, I tr into 3rd of 6 ch at beg of previous row, turn.

**Row 8**: 3 ch (counts as I tr), miss tr at base of 3 ch, *I tr into each of next 8 ch**, 8 ch, miss 8 tr, rep from * to end, ending last rep at **, I tr into 3rd of I I ch at beg of previous row, turn.

These 8 rows form patt.

Work in patt for a further 31 [35: 39] rows, ending after patt row 7 [3: 7]. Fasten off.

SLEEVES
Using 2.50mm (US B1/C2) crochet hook make 92 [108: 124] ch.
Work foundation row as given for back and front. 5½ [6½: 7½] patt reps.
Beg with patt row I, now work in patt as given for back and front for 15 rows, ending after patt row 7.
Fasten off.

MAKING UP
Press as described on the information page.

**Hem borders (make 2)**
Using 2.50mm (US B1/C2) crochet hook make 13 ch.
**Row I (RS):** (dtr3tog, 4 ch, I ttr, 4 ch and dtr3tog) into 9th ch from hook, miss 3 ch, I dtr into last ch, turn.

**Row 2:** 5 ch (counts as I ttr), miss (st at base of 5 ch, dtr3tog and 4 ch), (dtr3tog, 4 ch, I ttr, 4 ch and dtr3tog) into next ttr, miss (4 ch and dtr3tog), I ttr into top of 5 ch at beg of previous row, turn.
Rep last row until strip, unstretched, fits neatly across foundation ch of back and/or front, ending after a RS row – do NOT turn at end of last row.
Now work along one long row-end edge of strip as folls: I ch (does NOT count as st), 6 dc into first row-end edge (this is the ttr at end of previous row), 6 dc into each row-end edge to foundation ch edge of strip, adjusting number of sts worked so that you have a multiple of 4 dc plus one extra and ending with I dc into same foundation ch as ttr at beg of first row of strip, turn.
***Next row (WS):** I ch (does NOT count as st), I dc into first dc, *5 ch, miss 3 dc, I dc into next dc; rep from * to end, turn.
**Next row**: 4 ch (counts as I tr and I ch), miss dc at base of 4 ch, I dc into next ch sp, *4 ch, miss I dc, I dc into next ch sp; rep from * until dc has been worked into last ch sp, I ch, I tr into dc at beg of previous row, turn.
**Next row:** I ch (does NOT count as st), I dc into tr at base of I ch, I dc into next ch sp, *miss I dc**, (2 dc, 3 ch, ss to 3rd ch from hook, 2 dc) into next ch sp, rep from * to end, ending last rep at **, 2 dc into last ch sp.
Fasten off.

This completes lower side of border.
Now work along other side of strip as folls:
Attach yarn to base of "turning ch" at beg of first row of strip, I ch (does NOT count as st), 6 dc into first row-end edge (this is the 4 "turning ch" at beg of first row of strip), 6 dc into each row-end edge to end of strip, adjusting number of sts worked so that you have a multiple of 4 dc plus one extra and ending with I dc into top of turning ch at beg of last row of strip, turn.
Complete this side of border as given for first side from ***.

**Join hem border to body**
With RS facing and using 2.5mm (US B1/C2) crochet hook, attach yarn at bottom right hand edge of foundation row of back and/or front, 3 ch (counts as I tr), miss tr at base of 3 ch, I tr into each ch at base of next 8 tr, *5 tr into ch sp, I tr into each ch at base of next 8 tr; rep from * to last st, I tr into ch at base of last tr, turn. 114 [140: 166] sts.
**Next row:** 3 ch (counts as I tr), miss tr at base of 3 ch, I tr into each of next 3 [1: 2] tr, *I ch, miss I tr, I tr into each of next 2 tr; rep from * to last 5 [3: 4] sts, I ch, miss I tr, I tr into each of next 3 [1: 2] tr, I tr into top of 3 ch at beg of previous row.
Fasten off.
Neatly sew border to lower edge of back and/or front, by attaching each picot of hem border to a 2 ch sp on the back and/or front.
[Tip: If you prefer, the hem border can be attached to back and/or front by working a row of slip sts as follows: place WS of back and/or front to WS of hem border, join yarn to first st on back and/or front, 3 ch, ss into first st on border, ss along to first picot, ss into picot, I ch, ss into first ch sp on back and/or front, *(ss into each of next 2 tr and ch sp), I ch, ss into next picot on hem border, I ch, ss into same ch sp previously worked; rep from * to end, ending ss along to end of row after last ch sp on back and/or front, 3 ch, ss to last st on hem border.
Fasten off.

**Cuff borders (both alike)**
Work as given for hem border, making the original base strip slightly **shorter** than foundation ch edge of sleeve.

**Join cuff border to sleeve**
With RS facing and using 2.5mm (US B1/C2) crochet hook, attach yarn at bottom right hand edge of foundation row of sleeve, 3 ch (counts as I tr), miss tr at base of 3 ch, I tr into each ch at base of next 8 tr, *5 tr into ch sp, I tr into each ch at base of next 8 tr; rep from * to last st, I tr into ch at base of last tr, turn. 75 [88: 101] sts.
**Next row:** 3 ch (counts as I tr), miss tr at base of 3 ch, I tr into each of next 3 [2: 1] tr, *I ch, miss I tr, I tr into each of next 2 tr; rep from * to last 5 [4: 3] sts, I ch, miss I tr, I tr into each of next 3 [2: 1] tr, I tr into top of 3 ch at beg of previous row.
Fasten off.
Neatly sew cuff border to lower edge of sleeve, by attaching each picot of cuff border to a 2 ch sp on the sleeve.
Alternatively attach cuff border to sleeve with a ss row as stated in the join hem border to body tip.
Join shoulder seams by joining tops of last rows of back and front leaving 28 [29: 30] cm open at centre – this forms neck opening edge.
Mark points along side seam edges of back and front 16 [19: 21.5] cm

either side of shoulder seams. Sew top of last row of sleeves to back and front between these points, stretching top of sleeve slightly to fit. Join side and sleeve seams.

## Neck edging

With RS facing and using 2.50mm (US B1/C2) crochet hook, attach yarn at neck edge of one shoulder seam, 1 ch (does NOT count as st), now work 1 round of dc evenly around entre neck opening edge, working a multiple of 4 dc and ending with ss to first dc, turn.

**Next round (WS):** 1 ch (does NOT count as st), 1 dc into each of first 2 dc, *3 ch, ss to 3rd ch from hook, 1 dc into each of next 4 dc; rep from * to last 2 dc, 3 ch, ss to 3rd ch from hook, 1 dc into each of last 2 dc, ss to first dc.

Fasten off.

See information page for finishing instructions.

# ANEMONE ●●

| | S | M | L | XL | XXL | |
|---|---|---|---|---|---|---|
| To fit bust | 81-86 | 91-97 | 102-107 | 112-117 | 122-127 | cm |
| | 32-34 | 36-38 | 40-42 | 44-46 | 48-50 | in |

**Rowan Summerlite**

| | | | | | | |
|---|---|---|---|---|---|---|
| | 6 | 7 | 8 | 9 | 10 | x 50gm |

(photographed in Pure White 417)

## Needles

1 pair 2¼mm (no 13) (US 1) needles
1 pair 3mm (no 11) (US 2/3) needles
2.50mm (no 12) (US B1/C2) crochet hook

## Tension

28 sts and 36 rows to 10 cm measured over st st using 3mm (US 2/3) needles. Over sleeve patt, 36 sts (6 patt repeats) measure **14** cm and 20 rows (5 patt repeats) measure **12.5** cm using 2.50mm (US B1/C2) crochet hook.

## Crochet abbreviations

ch = chain; dc = double crochet; sp(s) = space(s); ss = slip stitch; tr = treble.

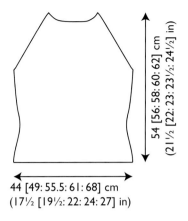

54 [56: 58: 60: 62] cm
(21½ [22: 23: 23½: 24½] in)

44 [49: 55.5: 61: 68] cm
(17½ [19½: 22: 24: 27] in)

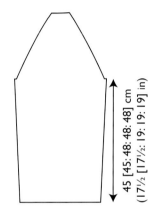

45 [45: 48: 48: 48] cm
(17½ [17½: 19: 19: 19] in)

BACK and FRONT (both alike)
Using 2¼mm (US 1) needles cast on 122 [138: 154: 170: 190] sts.
**Row 1 (RS):** K2, *P2, K2, rep from * to end.
**Row 2:** P2, *K2, P2, rep from * to end.
These 2 rows form rib.
Work in rib for a further 12 rows, ending with RS facing for next row.
Cont in rib, dec 1 st at each end of next and 2 foll 8th rows.
116 [132: 148: 164: 184] sts.
Work 1 row, inc [dec: inc: inc: inc] 1 st at centre of row and ending with RS facing for next row. 117 [131: 149: 165: 185] sts.
Change to 3mm (US 2/3) needles.
Beg with a K row, now work in st st throughout as folls:
Work 2 rows, ending with RS facing for next row.
**Next row (RS):** K4, sl 1, K1, psso, K to last 6 sts, K2tog, K4.
Working all side seam decreases as set by last row, dec 1 st at each end of 6th and foll 6th row. 111 [125: 143: 159: 179] sts.
Work 13 [13: 15: 15: 17] rows, ending with RS facing for next row.
**Next row (RS):** K5, M1, K to last 5 sts, M1, K5.

Working all side seam increases as set by last row, inc 1 st at each end of 8th and 4 foll 8th rows. 123 [137: 155: 171: 191] sts.
Cont straight until work meas 31 [32: 33: 34: 35] cm, ending with RS facing for next row.
**Shape raglan armholes**
Place markers at both ends of last row (to denote base of raglan armhole openings).
**Next row (RS):** K4, sl 1, K1, psso, K to last 6 sts, K2tog, K4.
**Next row:** P4, P2tog, P to last 6 sts, P2tog tbl, P4.
119 [133: 151: 167: 187] sts.
Working all raglan armhole decreases as set by last 2 rows, dec 1 st at each end of next 13 [23: 37: 49: 63] rows, then on foll 21 [18: 12: 8: 3] alt rows. 51 [51: 53: 53: 55] sts.
Work 1 row, ending with RS facing for next row.
Cast off.

SLEEVES
Using 2.50mm (US B1/C2) crochet hook make 51 [57: 57: 57: 57] ch.
**Foundation row (RS):** 1 dc into 2nd ch from hook, 1 dc into next ch, *6 ch, miss 4 ch, 1 dc into each of next 2 ch; rep from * to end, turn.
8 [9: 9: 9: 9] patt reps.
Now work in patt as folls:
**Row 1 (WS):** 3 ch (counts as 1 tr), miss dc at base of 3 ch, 1 tr into next dc, *2 ch, 1 dc into next ch sp, 2 ch, 1 tr into each of next 2 dc; rep from * to end, turn.
**Row 2:** 3 ch (counts as 1 tr), miss tr at base of 3 ch, 1 tr into next tr, *3 ch, miss 2 ch, 1 ss into next dc, 3 ch, miss 2 ch, 1 tr into each of next 2 tr; rep from * to end, working tr at end of last rep into top of 3 ch at beg of previous row, turn.
**Row 3:** 1 ch (does NOT count as st), 1 dc into each of first 2 tr, *4 ch, miss (3 ch, 1 ss and 3 ch), 1 dc into each of next 2 tr; rep from * to end, working dc at end of last rep into top of 3 ch at beg of previous row, turn.
**Row 4:** 1 ch (does NOT count as st), 1 dc into each of first 2 dc, *6 ch, miss 4 ch, 1 dc into each of next 2 dc; rep from * to end, turn.
These 4 rows form patt.
Now cont in patt and shape sleeve as folls:
**Row 5:** 3 ch (counts as 1 tr), 1 tr into dc at base of 3 ch, 1 tr into next dc, *2 ch, 1 dc into next ch sp, 2 ch**, 1 tr into each of next 2 dc; rep from * to end, ending last rep at **, 1 tr into next dc, 2 tr into last dc, turn.
**Row 6:** 3 ch (counts as 1 tr), 1 tr into tr at base of 3 ch, 1 tr into each of next 2 tr, *3 ch, miss 2 ch, 1 ss into next dc, 3 ch, miss 2 ch, 1 tr into each of next 2 tr; rep from * to last st, 2 tr into top of 3 ch at beg of previous row, turn.
**Row 7:** 1 ch (does NOT count as st), 2 dc into first tr, 1 dc into each of next 3 tr, *4 ch, miss (3 ch, 1 ss and 3 ch), 1 dc into each of next 2 tr; rep from * to last 2 sts, 1 dc into next tr, 2 dc into top of 3 ch at beg of previous row, turn.
**Row 8:** 1 ch (does NOT count as st), 2 dc into first dc, 1 dc into each of next 4 dc, *6 ch, miss 4 ch, 1 dc into each of next 2 dc; rep from * to last 3 sts, 1 dc into each of next 2 dc, 2 dc into last dc, turn.
**Row 9:** 3 ch (counts as 1 tr), 1 tr into dc at base of 3 ch, 1 tr into next dc, 2 ch, miss 2 dc, 1 tr into each of next 2 dc, *2 ch, 1 dc into next ch sp, 2

ch, I tr into each of next 2 dc; rep from * to last 4 dc, 2 ch, miss 2 dc, I tr into next dc, 2 tr into last dc, turn.

**Row 10:** 6 ch (counts as I tr and 3 ch), miss first 2 tr, I ss into next tr, 3 ch, miss 2 ch, I tr into each of next 2 tr, *3 ch, miss 2 ch, I ss into next dc, 3 ch, miss 2 ch, I tr into each of next 2 tr; rep from * to last 5 sts, 3 ch, miss 2 ch, I ss into next tr, 3 ch, miss I tr, I tr into top of 3 ch at beg of previous row, turn.

**Row 11:** I ch (does NOT count as st), 2 dc into first tr, *4 ch, miss (3 ch, I ss and 3 ch)**, I dc into each of next 2 tr; rep from * to end, ending last rep at **, 2 dc into top of 3 ch at beg of previous row, turn.

**Row 12:** I ch (does NOT count as st), I dc into each of first 2 dc, *6 ch, miss 4 ch, I dc into each of next 2 dc; rep from * to end, turn.
10 [11: 11: 11: 11] patt reps.

***Now work rows 1 to 4, 3 [3: 4: 2: 2] times, then rep rows 5 to 12 again. Rep from *** 1 [1: 1: 2: 2] times more. 14 [15: 15: 17: 17] patt reps.

Now work rows 1 to 4, 4 [4: 3: 3: 3] times more, and then rep row 1 **only** again. (Sleeve should meas approx 43 [43: 46: 46: 46] cm.)

### Shape raglan

Place markers at both ends of last row (to denote base of raglan armhole openings).

****Row 1: Ss across and into 5th st (this is dc at centre of first rep), 3 ch (does NOT count as st), miss 2 ch, I tr into each of next 2 tr, patt to last 7 sts, miss 2 ch, I tr into next dc and turn, leaving rem 4 sts unworked.

**Row 2:** I ch (does NOT count as st), miss tr at base of I ch, I dc into each of next 2 tr, patt to end, remembering 3 ch at beg of previous row does NOT count as a st, turn. 12 [13: 13: 15: 15] patt reps.
Work 2 rows.****

Rep last 4 rows 1 [2: 1: 2: 2] times more. 10 [9: 11: 11: 11] patt reps.
Work 4 rows, then rep from **** to **** once more. 8 [7: 9: 9: 9] patt reps.

### Sizes S, M, L and XXL only

Rep last 8 rows 1 [0: 1: -: 1] times more. 6 [7: 7: -: 7] patt reps.

### Size XL only

Work 4 rows, then work rows 1 and 2 **of raglan shaping** once more.
7 patt reps.

### All sizes

Work 2 [3: 3: 1: 3] rows, ending with row 3 [4: 4: 4: 4] **of patt**.

### Sizes M, L, XL and XXL only

**Next row:** Ss across and into centre of first ch sp, I ch (does NOT count as st), I dc into ch sp at base of I ch, 2 ch, I tr into each of next 2 dc, patt until dc has been worked into last ch sp and turn, leaving rem sts unworked. 6 patt reps.

### Sizes M and XL only

**Next row:** I ch (does NOT count as st), I dc into st at base of I ch, 2 ch, miss 2 ch, I tr into each of next 2 tr, patt until the 2 tr have been worked into last 2 tr, 2 ch, miss 2 ch, I dc into next dc, turn.

**Next row:** 4 ch (counts as I tr and I ch), miss st at base of 4 ch and next 2 ch, I dc into each of next 2 tr, patt until the 2 dc have been worked into last 2 tr, I ch, I tr into dc at beg of previous row.

### All sizes

Fasten off.

MAKING UP

Press as described on the information page.

Matching markers, join all raglan armhole seams using back stitch, or mattress stitch if preferred. (**Note:** Sleeve raglan edge may be very slightly longer or shorter than body raglan armhole edge so you will need to ease in the very slight fullness on the body or sleeves.)

### Neck edging

With RS facing and using 2.50mm (US B1/C2) crochet hook, attach yarn at top of left back raglan seam, I ch (does NOT count as st), work I row of dc evenly around entire neck edge, working a multiple of 4 dc and ending with ss to first dc, turn.

**Next round:** I ch (does NOT count as st), I dc into each dc to end, ss to first dc, turn.

**Next round:** I ch (does NOT count as st), I dc into each of first 2 dc, *3 ch, I ss into 3rd ch from hook**, I dc into each of next 4 dc, rep from * to end, ending last rep at **, I dc into each of last 2 dc, ss to first dc.
Fasten off.

Join side and sleeve seams.

### Cuff edgings (both alike)

Work as given for neck edging, attaching yarn at base of sleeve seam.
See information page for finishing instructions.

and draw through all 4 loops on hook.

## BACK

Using 2.50mm (US B1/C2) crochet hook make 143 [173] ch.
**Foundation row (RS):** (1 dtr, 4 ch and 1 dtr) into 7th ch from hook, *dtr2tog over next 6 ch working first "leg" into first of these 6 ch and 2nd "leg" into 6th of these 6 ch, 4 ch, 1 dtr into same ch as used for 2nd "leg" of previous dtr2tog; rep from * to last 4 ch, dtr2tog over these last 4 ch working first "leg" into first of these 4 ch and 2nd "leg" into 4th of these 4 ch, turn. 23 [28] patt reps.
Now work in patt as folls:
**Row 1:** 6 ch (counts as 1 dtr and 2 ch), 1 dtr into st at base of 6 ch, *dtr2tog over next 6 sts working first "leg" into next dtr and 2nd "leg" into next dtr2tog missing the 4 ch between**, 4 ch, 1 dtr into same st as used for last "leg" of previous dtr2tog; rep from * to end, ending last rep at ** and working 2nd "leg" of this dtr2tog into dtr at beg of previous row, 2 ch, 1 dtr into same st as used for last "leg" of previous dtr2tog, turn.

# P E O N Y  ● ● ●

|  | S-M | L-XL |
|---|---|---|
| To fit bust | 81-97 | 102-117 |
|  | 32-38 | 40-46 |

**Rowan Summerlite**

|  | 8 | 10 | × 50gm |
|---|---|---|---|

(photographed in Washed Linen 418)

## Crochet hook
2.50mm (no 12) (US B1/C2) crochet hook

## Tension
5 patt repeats to **10.5** cm and 9 rows to 10 cm measured over patt using 2.50mm (US B1/C2) crochet hook. Each motif measures 11.5 cm along each side, from corner to corner.

## Crochet abbreviations
**ch** = chain; **dc** = double crochet; **dtr** = double treble; **sp(s)** = space(s); **ss** = slip stitch; **tr** = treble; **yoh** = yarn over hook; **dtr2tog** = *(yoh) twice and insert hook as indicated, yoh and draw loop through, (yoh and draw through 2 loops) twice, rep from * once more, yoh and draw through all 3 loops on hook; **tr2tog** = (yoh and insert hook as indicated, yoh and draw loop through, yoh and draw through 2 loops) twice, yoh and draw through all 3 loops on hook; **tr3tog** = (yoh and insert hook as indicated, yoh and draw loop through, yoh and draw through 2 loops) 3 times, yoh

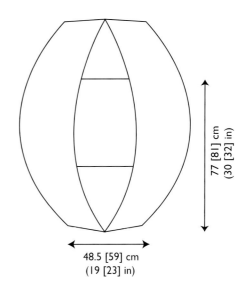

77 [81] cm (30 [32] in)

48.5 [59] cm (19 [23] in)

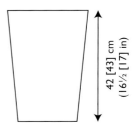

42 [43] cm (16½ [17] in)

**Row 2**: 4 ch (does NOT count as st), miss dtr at base of 4 ch and next 2 ch, 1 dtr into next dtr2tog, 4 ch, 1 dtr into same st at used for previous dtr, *dtr2tog over next 6 sts working first "leg" into next dtr and 2nd "leg" into next dtr2tog missing the 4 ch between**, 4 ch, 1 dtr into same st as used for last "leg" of previous dtr2tog; rep from * to end, ending last rep at ** but working 2nd "leg" of this dtr2tog into 4th of 6 ch at beg of previous row, turn.

These 2 rows form patt.

Cont in patt until back meas 30 [30]cm.

Fasten off.

## SLEEVES

### Main section

Using 2.50mm (US B1/C2) crochet hook make 65 [65] ch.

Work foundation row as given for back. 10 [10] patt reps.

Beg with row 1, work in patt as given for back for 2 rows.

Now beg sleeve shaping as folls:

**Row 3 (WS):** 8 ch (counts as 1 dtr and 4 ch), 1 dtr into st at base of 8 ch, *dtr2tog over next 6 sts working first "leg" into next dtr and 2nd "leg" into next dtr2tog missing the 4 ch between, 4 ch**, 1 dtr into same st

as used for last "leg" of previous dtr2tog; rep from * to end, ending last rep at ** and working 2nd "leg" of last dtr2tog into top of dtr at beg of previous row, 2 dtr into same place as last "leg" of last dtr2tog, turn.

**Row 4**: 6 ch (counts as 1 dtr and 2 ch), 1 dtr into st at base of 6 ch, *dtr2tog over next 6 sts working first "leg" into next dtr and 2nd "leg" into next dtr2tog missing the 4 ch between**, 4 ch, 1 dtr into same st as used for last "leg" of previous dtr2tog; rep from * to end, ending last rep at ** and working 2nd "leg" of this dtr2tog into 4th of 8 ch at beg of previous row, 2 ch, 1 dtr into same st as used for last "leg" of previous dtr2tog, turn. 11 [11] patt reps.

**Row 5**: As patt row 2.

Rep last 3 rows 2 [4] times more. 13 [15] patt reps.

Beg with patt row 1, work in patt for 2 rows.

Rep rows 3 to 5 once more. 14 [16] patt reps.

Rep last 5 rows 3 [2] times more. 17 [18] patt reps.

Beg with patt row 1, cont in patt until sleeve meas 39 [40] cm.

Fasten off.

### Cuff edging

With RS facing and using 2.50mm (US B1/C2) crochet hook, attach yarn to one end of foundation ch edge, 1 ch (does NOT count as st), work 65

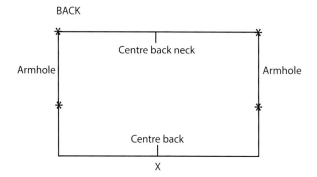

BACK

Centre back neck

Armhole · · · · · · · · · · · · · · · · · · · · · · · · · · · · Armhole

Centre back

X

dc evenly along foundation ch edge, turn.

**Row 1 (WS):** 3 ch (counts as 1 tr), 1 tr into st at base of 3 ch, *3 ch, miss 3 dc, 1 dc into next dc, 3 ch, ss to top of dc at base of 3 ch, 3 ch, miss 3 dc**, (1 tr, 2 ch and 1 tr) into next dc; rep from * to end, ending last rep at **, 2 tr into last dc, turn.

**Row 2:** 4 ch (counts as 1 tr and 1 ch), 1 tr into tr at base of 4 ch, *2 ch, miss (1 tr, 3 ch, 1 ss, 3 ch, 1 dc, 3 ch and 1 tr), (4 tr, 4 ch, ss to 4th ch from hook, 4 tr) into next ch sp, 2 ch, miss (1 tr, 3 ch, 1 ss, 3 ch, 1 dc, 3 ch and 1 tr)**, (1 tr, 5 ch, ss to 4th ch from hook, 1 ch and 1 tr) into next ch sp, rep from * to end, ending last rep at **, (1 tr, 1 ch and 1 tr) into top of 3 ch at beg of previous row.
Fasten off.

## BASIC MOTIF A

Using 2.50mm (US B1/C2) crochet hook make 4 ch and join with a ss to form a ring.

**Round 1 (RS):** 1 ch (does NOT count as st), 9 dc into ring, ss to first dc.

**Round 2:** 1 ch (does NOT count as st), 1 dc into st at base of 1 ch, (7 ch, miss 2 dc, 1 dc into next dc) twice, 3 ch, miss 2 dc, 1 dtr into top of dc at beg of round.

**Round 3:** 1 ch (does NOT count as st), 3 dc into ch sp partly formed by dtr at end of previous round, *1 dc into next dc, (3 dc, 3 ch and 3 dc into next ch sp; rep from * once more, 1 dc into next dc, 3 dc into next ch sp (this is same "ch" sp as used for the 3 dc at beg of round), 3 ch, ss to first dc.

**Round 4:** 3 ch (does NOT count as st), miss st at base of 3 ch, 1 tr into next dc, *1 tr into each of next 3 dc, tr2tog over next 2 dc, 7 ch, 1 dc into next ch sp, 7 ch, ss to 7th ch from hook, 7 ch**, tr2tog over next 2 dc; rep from * to end, ending last rep at **, ss to top of tr at beg of round (remembering the 3 ch do NOT count as a st).

**Round 5:** 3 ch (does NOT count as st), miss st at base of 3 ch, 1 tr into next tr, *1 tr into next tr, tr2tog over next 2 sts, 4 ch, 1 dc into next ch sp, 5 ch, 1 dc into next ch sp, 7 ch, ss to 7th ch from hook, 5 ch, 1 dc into next ch sp, 4 ch**, tr2tog over next 2 sts; rep from * to end, ending last rep at **, ss to top of tr at beg of round (remembering the 3 ch do NOT count as a st).

**Round 6:** 3 ch (does NOT count as st), miss st at base of 3 ch, tr2tog over next 2 sts, 3 ch, ss to 3rd ch from hook, *3 ch, 1 dc into next ch sp, (7 ch, 1 dc into next ch sp) twice, 7 ch, ss to 7th ch from hook, (7 ch, 1 dc into next ch sp) twice, 3 ch**, tr3tog over next 3 sts, 3 ch, ss to 3rd ch

SIZE S-M

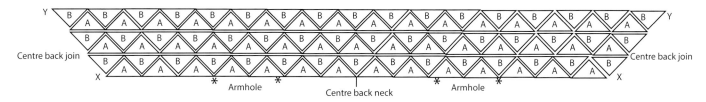

SIZE L-XL

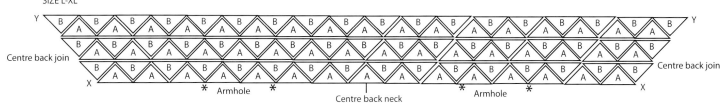

from hook; rep from * to end, ending last rep at **, ss to top of tr2tog at beg of round (remembering the 3 ch do NOT count as a st).
Fasten off.
Completed motif is a triangle. In each corner there is a 7-ch sp, and at centre of each side there is a 3-ch loop. Between corners and centre loop, there are a further two 7-ch sps. Join motifs whilst working round 6 by replacing each (7 ch) with (3 ch, I ss into corresponding ch sp of adjacent motif, 3 ch) and each (3 ch) with (I ch, I ss into corresponding ch loop of adjacent motif, I ch).

### BASIC MOTIF B

Using 2.50mm (US BI/C2) crochet hook make 4 ch and join with a ss to form a ring.

**Round I (RS):** 4 ch (counts as I dtr), 4 dtr into ring, (4 ch, 5 dtr into ring) twice, 4 ch, ss to top of 4 ch at beg of round.

**Round 2:** I ch (does NOT count as st), I dc into st at base of I ch, *(3 ch, I dc into next dtr) 4 times, 2 ch, I dc into next ch sp, 5 ch, ss to 5th ch from hook, 2 ch, I dc into next dtr; rep from * to end, replacing dc at end of last rep with ss to first dc.

**Round 3:** Ss across and into centre of first ch sp, I ch (does NOT count as st), I dc into ch sp at base of I ch, *(3 ch, I dc into next ch sp) 3 times, 4 ch, miss I ch sp, I dc into next ch sp, 5 ch, ss to 5th ch from hook, 4 ch, miss I ch sp, I dc into next ch sp; rep from * to end, replacing dc at end of last rep with ss to first dc.

**Round 4:** Ss across and into centre of first ch sp, I ch (does NOT count as st), I dc into ch sp at base of I ch, *(3 ch, I dc into next ch sp) twice, 7 ch, miss I ch sp, I dc into next ch sp, 5 ch, ss to 5th ch from hook, 7 ch, miss I ch sp, I dc into next ch sp; rep from * to end, replacing dc at end of last rep with ss to first dc.

**Round 5:** Ss across and into centre of first ch sp, I ch (does NOT count as st), I dc into ch sp at base of I ch, *4 ch, ss to **3rd** ch from hook, I ch, I dc into next ch sp, 7 ch, I dc into next ch sp, 7 ch, (I dc, 7 ch and I dc) into next ch sp, (7 ch, I dc into next ch sp) twice; rep from * to end,

replacing dc at end of last rep with ss to first dc.
Fasten off.
Completed motif is a triangle. In each corner there is a 7-ch sp, and at centre of each side there is a 3-ch loop. Between corners and centre loop, there are a further two 7-ch sps. Join motifs whilst working round 5 by replacing each (7 ch) with (3 ch, I ss into corresponding ch sp of adjacent motif, 3 ch) and each (3 ch) with (I ch, I ss into corresponding ch loop of adjacent motif, I ch).

### FRONT AND HEM MOTIF BORDER

Following diagram, make and join motifs A and B into a loop. There should be 14 [16] motifs A joined to 15 [17] motifs B.
Each foll band will contain one more of each motif and motifs A are always joined to motifs B and vice versa. Whilst making and joining motifs, also join ends of strips (as indicated on diagram by X and Y) so joined motifs form a pointed loop – where motifs join you will be joining motifs B to motifs B. You will need to make and join a total of 45 [51] motifs A and 48 [54] motifs B.

### MAKING UP

Press as described on the information page.
Mark points around outer edge of back as folls: Mark centre point of foundation ch edge – this point will match to point X on joined motif border. Mark centre of last row of back – this will match to centre 3-ch loop of central motif A of first band of motifs in border. Mark points along row-end edge of back 18 [20] cm down from top of last row – this indicates base of armhole openings (* - on diagram). Matching marked points, now sew front and hem border to back around all 4 edges, leaving open for armholes above row-end edge markers and top of back.
Join sleeve seams, then insert sleeves using the straight cast-off method – across front of sleeve, it will be attached to the motif border but across back of sleeve it will be attached to the back panel.
See information page for finishing instructions.

# LUPIN ● ●

| | S-M | L-XL | XXL | |
|---|---|---|---|---|
| To fit bust | 81-86 | 91-107 | 112-127 | cm |
| | 32-34 | 36-42 | 44-50 | in |

**Rowan Summerlite**

| | 10 | 13 | 15 | × 50gm |
|---|---|---|---|---|

(photographed in Pure White 417)

### Crochet hook
2.50mm (no 12) (US B1/C2) crochet hook

### Tension
26 sts and 16 rows to 10 cm measured over patt using 2.50mm (US B1/C2) crochet hook. Each motif measures approx 9 cm square.

### Crochet abbreviations
**ch** = chain; **dc** = double crochet; **dtr** = double treble; **qtr** = quadruple treble; **sp(s)** = space(s); **ss** = slip stitch; **tr** = treble; **yoh** = yarn over hook; **dc2tog** = (insert hook as indicated, yoh and draw loop through) twice, yoh and draw through all 3 loops on hook; **dtr3tog** = *(yoh) twice and insert hook as indicated, yoh and draw loop through, (yoh and draw through 2 loops) twice, rep from * twice more, yoh and draw through all 4 loops on hook; **tr2tog** = (yoh and insert hook as indicated, yoh and draw loop through, yoh and draw through 2 loops) twice, yoh and draw through all 3 loops on hook.

## BASIC MOTIF
Using 2.50mm (US B1/C2) crochet hook make 8 ch and join with a ss to form a ring.

**Round 1 (RS):** 1 ch (does NOT count as st), 16 dc into ring, ss to first dc.

**Round 2:** 1 ch (does NOT count as st), 1 dc into st at base of 1 ch, (7 ch, miss 3 dc, 1 dc into next dc) 3 times, 3 ch, 1 dtr into first dc.

**Round 3:** 3 ch (counts as 1 tr), (1 tr, 3 ch and 2 tr) into ch sp partly formed by dtr at end of previous row, *3 ch, tr2tog working first "leg" into ch sp just used and 2nd "leg" into next ch sp missing the dc between, 3 ch**, (2 tr, 3 ch and 2 tr) into ch sp just used for 2nd "leg" of tr2tog just worked; rep from * to end, ending last rep at **, ss to top of 3 ch at beg of round.

**Round 4:** Ss across and into first ch sp, 3 ch (counts as 1 tr), (1 tr, 3 ch and 2 tr) into same ch sp, *3 ch, miss 2 tr, 3 tr into next ch sp, 1 tr into next tr2tog, 3 tr into next ch sp, 3 ch**, miss 2 tr, (2 tr, 3 ch and 2 tr) into next ch sp; rep from * to end, ending last rep at **, ss to top of 3 ch at beg of round.

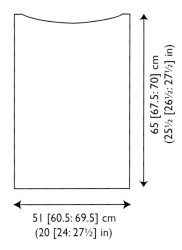

65 [67.5: 70] cm
(25½ [26½: 27½] in)

51 [60.5: 69.5] cm
(20 [24: 27½] in)

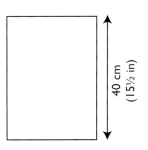

40 cm
(15½ in)

**Round 5**: Ss across and into first ch sp, 3 ch (counts as 1 tr), (2 tr, 3 ch and 3 tr) into same ch sp, *6 ch, miss (2 tr, 3 ch and 1 tr), 1 tr into each of next 5 tr, 6 ch, miss (1 tr, 3 ch and 2 tr)**, (3 tr, 3 ch and 3 tr) into next ch sp; rep from * to end, ending last rep at **, ss to top of 3 ch at beg of round.

**Round 6**: 3 ch (counts as 1 tr), miss st at base of 3 ch, 1 tr into each of next 2 tr, *(3 tr, 5 ch and 3 tr) into next ch sp, 1 tr into each of next 3 tr, 6 ch, miss (6 ch and 1 tr), 1 tr into each of next 3 tr, 6 ch, miss (1 tr and 6 ch)**, 1 tr into each of next 3 tr; rep from * to end, ending last rep at **, ss to top of 3 ch at beg of round.
Fasten off.
Completed motif is a square. In each corner there is a 5-ch sp, and there are a further two 6-ch sps along sides. Between corner ch sp and next ch sp there are 6 tr, and there are 3 tr at centre of each side.

BACK and FRONT (both alike)
**Motif band**
Make and join 5 [6: 7] motifs to form a strip. Join motifs with RS together as folls: attach yarn to one corner ch sp of first motif, 3 ch (counts as 1 tr), 1 ss into corresponding corner ch sp of 2nd motif, 1 tr into same ch sp of first motif, 1 ss into corresponding ch sp of 2nd motif, (1 tr into next tr along side of first motif, 1 ss into corresponding tr along side of 2nd motif) 6 times, 1 tr into next ch sp of first motif, 1 ss into next ch sp of 2nd motif, (1 tr into same ch sp as last tr on first motif, 1 ss into same ch sp as last ss on 2nd motif) twice, (1 tr into next tr along side of first motif, 1 ss into corresponding tr along side of 2nd motif) 3 times, 1 tr into next ch sp of first motif, 1 ss into next ch sp of 2nd motif, (1 tr into same ch sp as last tr on first motif, 1 ss into same ch sp as last ss on 2nd motif) twice, (1 tr into next tr along side of first motif, 1 ss into corresponding tr along side of 2nd motif) 6 times, 1 tr into next (corner) ch sp of first motif, 1 ss into next (corner) ch sp of 2nd motif, 1 tr into same ch sp as last tr on first motif, 1 ss into same ch sp as last ss on 2nd motif.
Fasten off.

**Lower body (worked downwards)**
With RS facing and using 2.50mm (US B1/C2) crochet hook, attach yarn to corner ch sp of motif band and work along long edge of band as folls: 1 ch (does NOT count as st), 2 dc into first corner ch sp (where yarn is attached), *1 dc into each of next 6 tr, 3 dc into next ch sp, 1 dc into each of next 3 tr, 3 dc into next ch sp, 1 dc into each of next 6 tr, 2 dc into next corner ch sp**, 1 dc into row-end of motif joining row, 2 dc into corner ch sp of next motif; rep from * to end, ending last rep at **, turn. 129 [155: 181] sts.
**Next row (WS)**: 1 ch (does NOT count as st), 1 dc into each dc to end, inc 4 [2: 0] dc evenly across row (by working 2 dc into 1 dc), turn. 133 [157: 181] sts.***
Now work in patt as folls:
**Row 1 (RS)**: 1 ch (does NOT count as st), 1 dc into each dc to end, turn.
**Row 2**: 7 ch (counts as 1 qtr and 1 ch), miss first 2 dc, 1 qtr into next dc, *1 ch, miss 1 dc, 1 qtr into next dc; rep from * to end, turn.
**Row 3**: 1 ch (does NOT count as st), 1 dc into qtr at base of 1 ch, *1 dc into next ch sp, 1 dc into next qtr; rep from * to end, working dc at end of last rep into 6th of 7 ch at beg of previous row, turn.

**Rows 4 and 5**: As row 1.
**Row 6**: 4 ch (counts as 1 dtr), miss st at base of 4 ch and next 2 dc, *(dtr3tog, 5 ch and dtr3tog) into next dc**, miss 5 dc; rep from * to end, ending last rep at **, miss 2 dc, 1 dtr into last dc, turn. 22 [26: 30] patt reps.
**Row 7**: 1 ch (does NOT count as st), 1 dc between dtr and dtr3tog at end of previous row, *miss 1 dtr3tog, 5 dc into next ch sp, miss 1 dtr3tog, 1 dc between dtr3tog just missed and next dtr3tog; rep from * to end, working dc at end of last rep between dtr3tog and turning ch, turn.
**Row 8**: As row 1.
These 8 rows form patt.
Work in patt for a further 49 [53: 57] rows, ending after patt row 1 [5: 1].
Fasten off.
**Upper body (worked upwards)**
Working along other long edge of motif band, work as given for lower body to ***.
Beg with patt row 5, now work in patt as given for lower body as folls:
Work 24 rows, ending after patt row 4.
**Shape neck**
**Row 1 (RS)**: 1 ch (does NOT count as st), 1 dc into each of first 31 [43: 55] dc and turn, leaving rem sts unworked.
Work a further 7 rows on these 31 [43: 55] sts (5 [7: 9] patt reps), ending after patt row 4.
Fasten off.
Return to last complete row worked, miss centre 71 dc, attach yarn to next st and cont as folls:
**Row 1 (RS)**: 1 ch (does NOT count as st), 1 dc into each dc to end, turn. 31 [43: 55] sts.
Work a further 7 rows on these 31 [43: 55] sts (5 [7: 9] patt reps), ending after patt row 4.
Fasten off.

SLEEVES
**Motif bands (make 2 for each sleeve)**
Make and join 4 motifs to form a strip, joining motifs in same way as for motif band of back and front.
**Centre joining band**
****With RS facing and using 2.50mm (US B1/C2) crochet hook, attach yarn to corner ch sp of one motif band and work along long edge of band as folls: 1 ch (does NOT count as st), 2 dc into first corner ch sp (where yarn is attached), *1 dc into each of next 6 tr, 3 dc into next ch sp, 1 dc into each of next 3 tr, 3 dc into next ch sp, 1 dc into each of next 6 tr, 2 dc into next corner ch sp**, 1 dc into row-end of motif joining row, 2 dc into corner ch sp of next motif; rep from * to end, ending last rep at **, turn. 103 sts.
**Row 1 (WS)**: 1 ch (does NOT count as st), 1 dc into each dc to end, turn.
**Row 2**: As row 1.
**Row 3**: 7 ch (counts as 1 qtr and 1 ch), miss first 2 dc, 1 qtr into next dc, *1 ch, miss 1 dc, 1 qtr into next dc; rep from * to end, turn.
**Row 4**: 1 ch (does NOT count as st), 1 dc into qtr at base of 1 ch, *1 dc into next ch sp, 1 dc into next qtr; rep from * to end, working dc at end of last rep into 6th of 7 ch at beg of previous row, turn.****
Rep last 4 rows 1 [2: 1] times more, and then row 1 again.

Fasten off.

With RS facing and using 2.50mm (US B1/C2) crochet hook, attach yarn to corner ch sp of other motif band and work along long edge of band as folls: 1 ch (does NOT count as st), 2 dc into first corner ch sp (where yarn is attached), *1 dc into each of next 6 tr, 3 dc into next ch sp, 1 dc into each of next 3 tr, 3 dc into next ch sp, 1 dc into each of next 6 tr, 2 dc into next corner ch sp**, 1 dc into row-end of motif joining row, 2 dc into corner ch sp of next motif; rep from * to end, ending last rep at **, turn. 103 sts.

Holding motif bands with RS together, now join this last row of dc on this second band to last row of dc on first band by working a row of ss, working each ss into 1 dc from each edge together.

Fasten off.

### Side bands (both alike)

Work along free edge of one motif band as given for centre joining band from **** to ****.

Rep last 4 rows 0 [0: 1] times more, and then row 1 again.

Fasten off.

MAKING UP

Press as described on the information page.

Join shoulder seams of upper body sections.

### Neck edging

With RS facing and using 2.50mm (US B1/C2) crochet hook, attach yarn at top of left shoulder seam, 1 ch (does NOT count as st), work 1 round of dc evenly around entire neck edge, ending with ss to first dc, turn.

**Next round**: 1 ch (does NOT count as st), 1 dc into each dc to end, working dc2tog either side of neck corner points and ending with ss to first dc.

Fasten off.

Measure 15 [16.5; 18]cm down from shoulder seam and place a marker. Matching centre of sleeve joining band to shoulder seam and stretching edge slightly, sew row-end edge of sleeve to back and front. Join side and sleeve seams.

### Shoulder straps (both alike)

Using 2.50mm (US B1/C2) crochet hook make 22 ch.

**Row 1 (RS):** 1 dc into 2nd ch from hook, 1 dc into each ch to end, turn. 21 sts.

**Row 2:** 1 ch (does NOT count as st), 1 dc into each dc to end, turn.

Rep last row once more.

Fasten off.

Attach ends of shoulder straps to inside of garment along neck opening line, positioning straps 3 cm in from top of sleeve/shoulder seam.

### Cuff edgings (both alike)

With RS facing and using 2.50mm (US B1/C2) crochet hook, attach yarn at base of sleeve seam, 1 ch (does NOT count as st), work 1 round of dc evenly around entire cuff opening edge, ending with ss to first dc, turn.

**Next round**: 1 ch (does NOT count as st), 1 dc into each dc to end, ending with ss to first dc.

Fasten off.

See information page for finishing instructions.

Row 1 (RS): K1, *P1, K1, rep from * to end.
Row 2: P1, *K1, P1, rep from * to end.
These 2 rows form rib.
Work in rib for a further 10 [10: 20: 20: 20] rows, ending with RS facing for next row.
**Next row (RS):** Rib 4, sl 1, K1, psso, rib to last 6 sts, K2tog, rib 4.
Working all side seam decreases as set by last row, dec 1 st at each end of 6th [6th: 8th: 8th: 8th] and 2 [3: 0: 0: 0] foll 6th [4th: -: -: -] rows.
115 [127: 151: 167: 187] sts.
Work 1 row, ending with RS facing for next row. (32 rows of rib completed).
Change to 3mm (US 2/3) needles.
Beg with a K row, now work in st st throughout as folls:
Work 2 [2: 6: 6: 6] rows, ending with RS facing for next row.
**Next row (RS):** K4, sl 1, K1, psso, K to last 6 sts, K2tog, K4.
Working all side seam decreases as set by last row, dec 1 [-: 1: 1: 1] st at each end of 4th [-: 8th: 8th: 8th] and 0 [-: 2: 2: 2] foll - [-: 8th: 8th: 8th] rows. 111 [125: 143: 159: 179] sts.
Work 13 rows, ending with RS facing for next row.
**Next row (RS):** K5, M1, K to last 5 sts, M1, K5.

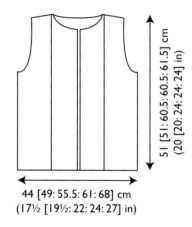

51 [51: 60.5: 60.5: 61.5] cm
(20 [20: 24: 24: 24] in)

44 [49: 55.5: 61: 68] cm
(17½ [19½: 22: 24: 27] in)

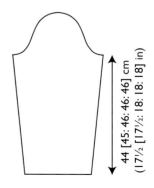

44 [45: 46: 46: 46] cm
(17½ [17½: 18: 18: 18] in)

# B U T T E R C U P ●●

| | S | M | L | XL | XXL | |
|---|---|---|---|---|---|---|
| To fit bust | 81-86 | 91-97 | 102-107 | 112-117 | 122-127 | cm |
| | 32-34 | 36-38 | 40-42 | 44-46 | 48-50 | in |
| **Rowan Summerlite** | 6 | 7 | 9 | 10 | 11 | × 50gm |

(photographed in Washed Linen 418)

## Needles and crochet hook
1 pair 2¼mm (no 13) (US 1) needles
1 pair 3mm (no 11) (US 2/3) needles
2.50mm (no 12) (US B1/C2) crochet hook

## Buttons – 8 [8: 9: 9: 9]

## Tension
28 sts and 36 rows to 10 cm measured over st st using 3mm (US 2/3) needles. Crochet motif is 8.5 cm square using 2.50mm (US B1/C2) crochet hook.

## Crochet abbreviations
**ch** = chain; **dc** = double crochet; **sp(s)** = space(s); **ss** = slip stitch; **tr** = treble.

## BACK
Using 2¼mm (US 1) needles cast on 123 [137: 155: 171: 191] sts.

Working all side seam increases as set by last row, inc 1 st at each end of 8th and 4 foll 8th rows. 123 [137: 155: 171: 191] sts.

Cont straight until back meas 30 [29: 37.5: 36.5: 36.5] cm, ending with RS facing for next row.

## Shape armholes

Cast off 5 [6: 7: 8: 9] sts at beg of next 2 rows.

113 [125: 141: 155: 173] sts.

**Next row (RS):** K4, sl 1, K1, psso, K to last 6 sts, K2tog, K4.

**Next row:** P4, P2tog, P to last 6 sts, P2tog tbl, P4.

Working all armhole decreases as set by last 2 rows, dec 1 st at each end of next 3 [5: 7: 9: 11] rows, then on foll 3 [4: 6: 7: 9] alt rows, then on foll 4th row. 95 [101: 109: 117: 127] sts.

Cont straight until armhole meas 18 [19: 20: 21: 22] cm, ending with RS facing for next row.

## Shape shoulders and back neck

Cast off 3 [3: 4: 5: 6] sts at beg of next 2 rows. 89 [95: 101: 107: 115] sts.

**Next row (RS):** Cast off 3 [4: 4: 5: 6] sts, K until there are 20 [22: 25: 27: 30] sts on right needle and turn, leaving rem sts on a holder.

Work each side of neck separately.

Dec 1 st at neck edge of next 6 rows **and at same time** cast off 3 [4: 4: 5: 6] sts at beg of 2nd and foll 1 [2: 0: 2: 2] alt rows, then 4 [-: 5: -: -] sts at beg of foll 1 [-: 2: -: -] alt rows.

Work 1 row.

Cast off rem 4 [4: 5: 6: 6] sts.

With RS facing, rejoin yarn and cast off centre 43 sts, K to end.

Complete to match first side, reversing shapings.


LEFT FRONT

## Side panel

Using 2¼mm (US 1) needles cast on 34 [42: 50: 58: 68] sts.

**Row 1 (RS):** *K1, P1, rep from * to last 2 sts, K2.

**Row 2:** *K1, P1, rep from * to end.

These 2 rows form rib.

Work in rib for a further 10 [10: 20: 20: 20] rows, ending with RS facing for next row.

**Next row (RS):** Rib 4, sl 1, K1, psso, rib to end.

Working all side seam decreases as set by last row, dec 1 st at beg of 6th [6th: 8th: 8th: 8th] and 2 [3: 0: 0: 0] foll 6th [4th: -: -: -] rows.

30 [37: 48: 56: 66] sts.

Work 1 row, dec 0 [1: 0: 0: 0] st at centre of row and ending with RS facing for next row. 30 [36: 48: 56: 66] sts.

Change to 3mm (US 2/3) needles.

**Next row (RS):** Knit.

**Next row:** K1, P to end.

These 2 rows set the sts – front opening edge st worked as a K st on every row with all other sts in st st.

Keeping sts correct as now set, cont as folls:

Work 0 [0: 4: 4: 4] rows, ending with RS facing for next row.

**Next row (RS):** K4, sl 1, K1, psso, K to end.

Working all side seam decreases as set by last row, dec 1 [-: 1: 1: 1] st at beg of 4th [-: 8th: 8th: 8th] and 0 [-: 2: 2: 2] foll – [-: 8th: 8th: 8th] rows.

28 [35: 44: 52: 62] sts.

Work 13 rows, ending with RS facing for next row.

**Next row (RS):** K5, M1, K to end.

Working all side seam increases as set by last row, inc 1 st at beg of 8th and 4 foll 8th rows. 34 [41: 50: 58: 68] sts.

Cont straight until left front matches back to beg of armhole shaping, ending with RS facing for next row.

## Shape armhole

Cast off 5 [6: 7: 8: 9] sts at beg of next row. 29 [35: 43: 50: 59] sts.

Work 1 row.

Working all armhole decreases as set by back, dec 1 st at armhole edge of next 5 [7: 9: 11: 13] rows, then on foll 3 [4: 6: 7: 9] alt rows, then on foll 4th row. 20 [23: 27: 31: 36] sts.

Cont straight until left front matches back to beg of shoulder shaping, ending with RS facing for next row.

## Shape shoulder

Cast off 3 [3: 4: 5: 6] sts at beg of next and foll 3 [0: 2: 4: 4] alt rows, then 4 [4: 5: -: -] sts at beg of foll 1 [4: 2: -: -] alt rows.

Work 1 row.

Cast off rem 4 [4: 5: 6: 6] sts.

**Centre front crochet panel**

Using 2.50mm (US B1/C2) crochet hook make 5 ch and join with a ss to form a ring.

**Round 1 (RS):** 3 ch (counts as 1 tr), 4 tr into ring, (3 ch, 5 tr into ring) 3 times, 3 ch, ss to top of 3 ch at beg of round.

**Round 2:** Ss across and into first tr of previous round, 3 ch (counts as 1 tr), 1 tr into each of next 2 tr, *4 ch, miss 1 tr, 1 tr into next ch sp, 4 ch, miss 1 tr**, 1 tr into each of next 3 tr; rep from * to end, ending last rep at **, ss to top of 3 ch at beg of round.

**Round 3:** Ss across and into first tr of previous round, 9 ch (counts as 1 tr and 6 ch), *miss (1 tr and 4 ch), (1 tr, 5 ch and 1 tr) into next tr, 6 ch, miss (4 ch and 1 tr)**, 1 tr into next tr, 6 ch; rep from * to end, ending last rep at **, ss to 3rd of 9 ch at beg of round.

**Round 4:** 1 ch (does NOT count as st), 1 dc into st at base of 1 ch, *5 ch, ss to dc at base of 5 ch, 5 ch, miss (6 ch and 1 tr), (3 tr, 5 ch, ss to tr at base of 5 ch, 2 tr, 5 ch, 2 tr, 5 ch, ss to tr at base of 5 ch, 3 tr) into next ch sp, 5 ch, miss (1 tr and 6 ch), 1 dc into next tr; rep from * to end, replacing dc at end of last rep with ss to first dc.

Fasten off.

Completed basic motif is a square. In each corner there is a 5-ch loop and there are three 5-ch picots along each side. Join motifs whilst working round 4 by replacing these (5 ch) with (2 ch, 1 ss into corresponding ch loop of adjacent motif, 2 ch) – motifs will be joined at 5 points along each joining edge.

Make and join 5 [5: 6: 6: 6] basic motifs to form a strip of motifs.


RIGHT FRONT

Using 2¼mm (US 1) needles cast on 34 [42: 50: 58: 68] sts.

**Row 1 (RS):** K2, *P1, K1, rep from * to end.

**Row 2:** *P1, K1, rep from * to end.

These 2 rows form rib.

Work in rib for a further 10 [10: 20: 20: 20] rows, ending with RS facing for next row.

**Next row (RS):** Rib to last 6 sts, K2tog, rib 4.

Working all side seam decreases as set by last row, dec 1 st at end of 6th [6th: 8th: 8th: 8th] and 2 [3: 0: 0: 0] foll 6th [4th: -: -: -] rows. 30 [37: 48: 56: 66] sts.

Work 1 row, dec 0 [1: 0: 0: 0] st at centre of row and ending with RS facing for next row. 30 [36: 48: 56: 66] sts.

# C A R N A T I O N ●●

|  | S-M | L-XL | XXL |  |
|---|---|---|---|---|
| To fit bust | 81-86 | 91-107 | 112-127 | cm |
|  | 32-34 | 36-42 | 44-50 | in |

**Rowan Summerlite**

|  |  | 9 | 11 | 13 | x 50gm |
|---|---|---|---|---|---|

(photographed in Washed Linen 418)

## Needles and crochet hook
1 pair 2¼mm (no 13) (US 1) needles
2.50mm (no 12) (US B1/C2) crochet hook

**Buttons** - 1

Change to 3mm (US 2/3) needles.

**Next row (RS):** Knit.

**Next row:** P to last st, K1.

These 2 rows set the sts – front opening edge st worked as a K st on every row with all other sts in st st.

Keeping sts correct as now set, cont as folls:

## Tension
Each motif measures 7.5 cm square **before joining** using 2.50mm (US B1/C2) crochet hook. 35 sts and 44 rows to 10 cm measured over rib when slightly stretched using 2¼mm (US 1) needles.

## Crochet abbreviations
**ch** = chain; **dc** = double crochet; **htr** = half treble; **sp(s)** = space(s); **ss** = slip stitch; **tr** = treble; **ttr** = triple treble; **yoh** = yarn over hook; **tr2tog** = (yoh and insert hook as indicated, yoh and draw loop through, yoh and draw through 2 loops) twice, yoh and draw through all 3 loops on hook; **dtr2tog** = *(yoh) twice and insert hook as indicated, yoh and draw loop through, (yoh and draw through 2 loops) twice; rep from * once more, yoh and draw through all 3 loops on hook.

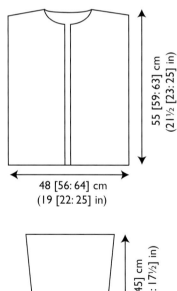

55 [59: 63] cm (21½ [23: 25] in)

48 [56: 64] cm (19 [22: 25] in)

44 [45: 45] cm (17½ [17½: 17½] in)

## BASIC MOTIF

Using 2.50mm (US B1/C2) crochet hook make 5 ch and join with a ss to form a ring.

**Round 1 (RS):** 1 ch (does NOT count as st), (1 dc into ring, 3 ch) 4 times, ss to first dc.

**Round 2:** Ss into first ch sp, 3 ch (counts as 1 tr), 4 tr into same ch sp as used for ss, *2 ch, miss 1 dc**, 5 tr into next ch sp; rep from * to end, ending last rep at **, ss to top of 3 ch at beg of round.

**Round 3:** 1 ch (does NOT count as st), 1 dc into st at base of 1 ch, *(3 ch, 1 dc into next tr) 4 times**, 5 ch, miss 2 ch, 1 dc into next tr; rep from * to end, ending last rep at **, 2 ch, 1 tr into dc at beg of round.

**Round 4:** 1 ch (does NOT count as st), 1 dc into ch sp partly formed by tr at end of previous round, *3 ch, 1 dc into next ch sp; rep from * to end, replacing dc at end of last rep with ss to first dc. 20 ch sps.

**Round 5:** 5 ch (counts as 1 tr and 2 ch), 1 tr into st at base of 5 ch, *3 ch, miss (3 ch and 1 dc), 1 dc into next ch sp, (3 ch, miss 1 dc, 1 dc into next ch sp) twice, 3 ch, miss (1 dc and 3 ch)**, (1 tr, 2 ch and 1 tr) into next dc; rep from * to end, ending last rep at **, ss to 3rd of 5 ch at beg of round.

**Round 6:** Ss into first ch sp, 3 ch (does NOT count as st), (1 tr, 3 ch, tr2tog, 3 ch and tr2tog) into ch sp at base of 3 ch, *4 ch, miss (1 tr, 3 ch and 1 dc), 1 dc into next ch sp, 3 ch, miss 1 dc, 1 dc into next ch sp, 4 ch, miss (1 dc, 3 ch and 1 tr)**, (tr2tog, 3 ch, tr2tog, 3 ch and tr2tog) into next ch sp; rep from * to end, ending last rep at **, ss to top of first tr (remembering the 3 ch does NOT count as a st).

**Round 7:** Ss into centre of first ch sp, 1 ch (does NOT count as st), 1 dc into ch sp at base of 1 ch, *7 ch, miss tr2tog, 1 dc into next ch sp, 7 ch, miss (tr2tog, 4 ch and 1 dc), 1 dc into next ch sp, 7 ch, miss (1 dc, 4 ch and tr2tog), 1 dc into next ch sp; rep from * to end, replacing dc at end of last rep with ss to first dc.
Fasten off.

Basic motif is a square. In each corner, there is a loop of 7 ch and there are a further two loops of 7 ch along each side between corner loops. Join motifs into strips by working a row of tr and ss as folls: attach yarn to one corner ch sp of first motif, 3 ch (counts as 1 tr), holding motifs with RS together work 1 ss into corresponding corner ch sp of adjacent motif (2nd motif), (1 tr into same corner ch sp of first motif, 1 ss into same corner ch sp of 2nd motif) twice, *1 tr into next (side) ch sp of first motif, 1 ss into corresponding (side) ch sp of 2nd motif, (1 tr into same ch sp of first motif, 1 ss into same corner ch sp of 2nd motif) 4 times; rep from * once more, 1 tr into next (corner) ch sp of first motif, 1 ss into corresponding (corner) ch sp of 2nd motif, (1 tr into same ch sp of first motif, 1 ss into same corner ch sp of 2nd motif) twice.
Once all strips have been made, join strips to each other in same way, working 1 tr into joining row of first strip and 1 ss into corresponding joining row of next strip.

## BODY

### Main section

Make 70 [82: 110] basic motifs.
Following appropriate diagram, now join motifs to form shape shown in diagram for appropriate size. Once shape is complete, join shoulder seams by working the joining row across upper edge of back section, attaching shoulder edges of fronts to back as indicated on diagram. (**Note:** On size L-XL, actual shoulder fold line will fall along centre of shoulder motifs.)

### Hem border

With RS facing and using 2.50mm (no 12) crochet hook, join yarn to corner ch sp on lower (hem) edge of motifs, 1 ch (does NOT count as st), *2 dc into same corner ch sp, work [1 dc into next dc, 5 dc into next ch sp] twice, 1 dc into next dc, 2 dc into corner ch sp **, 2 dc across the tr join between the motifs; rep from * to end, ending last rep at **, turn.

**Next row (WS):** 1 ch (does NOT count as st), 1 dc into each dc to end. 226 [264: 302] sts.
Fasten off.
With RS facing and using 2¼mm (US 1) needles, pick up and knit 338 [394: 450] sts evenly along lower (hem) edge of motifs.

**Row 1 (WS):** *P2, K2; rep from * to last 2 sts, P2.
**Row 2:** *K2, P2; rep from * to last 2 sts, K2.
These 2 rows form rib.
Cont in rib until hem border meas 7 cm **from pick-up row**, ending with RS facing for next row.
Cast off in rib.

## SLEEVES

Using 2¼mm (US 1) needles cast on 62 [70: 74] sts.
**Row 1 (RS):** K2, *P2, K2; rep from * to end.
**Row 2:** P2, *K2, P2; rep from * to end.
These 2 rows form rib.
Cont in rib, shaping sides by inc 1 st at each end of 5th [3rd: next] and every foll 6th [4th: alt] row to 90 [104: 86] sts, then on every foll 8th [6th: 4th] row until there are 112 [140: 168] sts, taking inc sts into rib.
Cont straight until sleeve meas 44 [45: 45] cm, ending with RS facing for next row.

### Size L-XL only

Place markers at both ends of last row.
Work a further 16 rows, ending with RS facing for next row.

### All sizes

Cast off in rib.

## MAKING UP

Press as described on the information page.

### Neck filling triangles (make 2 [4: 2])

At inner corners of joined motifs indicated by A on diagram, mark 9th st away from actual corner, counting along edge of "joining" row.
With RS facing and using 2.50mm (US B1/C2) crochet hook, attach yarn to this st and work around inner corner as folls: 1 ss into point where yarn was attached, 1 dc into each of next 2 sts, 1 htr into each of next 2 sts, 1 tr into each of next 2 sts, dtr2tog over next 2 sts, 1 ttr into corner, then work along next edge as folls: dtr2tog over first 2 sts, 1 tr into each of next 2 sts, 1 htr into each of next 2 sts, 1 dc into each of next 2 sts, 1 ss into next st.
Fasten off.

### Left front band

With RS facing and using 2.50mm (US B1/C2) crochet hook, attach yarn at neck edge of left front opening edge, 1 ch (does NOT count as st), work 1 row of dc evenly down entire left front opening edge, ending at

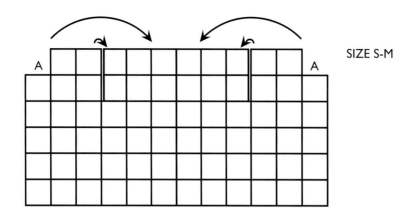

SIZE S-M

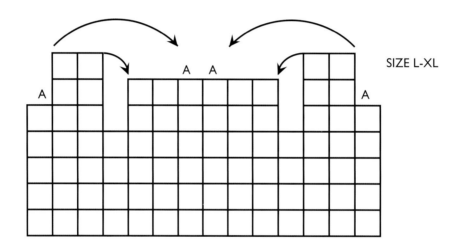

SIZE L-XL

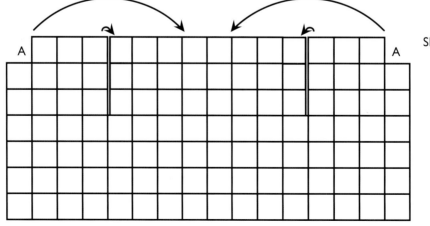

SIZE XXL

cast-off edge of hem border, turn.

**Next row (WS):** 1 ch (does NOT count as st), 1 dc into each dc to end. Fasten off.

### Right front band

With RS facing and using 2.50mm (US B1/C2) crochet hook, attach yarn at base (cast-off edge of hem border) of right front opening edge, 1 ch (does NOT count as st), work 1 row of dc evenly up entire right front opening edge, ending at neck edge, turn.

**Next row (WS):** 1 ch (does NOT count as st), 1 dc into first dc, 4 ch, miss 2 dc (this forms button loop), 1 dc into each dc to end. Fasten off.

### Collar

With RS facing and using 2¼mm (US 1) needles, beg and ending at centre of front bands, pick up and knit 49 [63: 49] sts up right side of front neck, 58 [94: 58] sts from back neck, and 49 [63: 49] sts down left side of front neck. 156 [220: 156] sts.

**Row 1 (WS of body, RS of collar):** K3, *P2, K2; rep from * to last st, K1. This row sets position of rib as given for hem border, but with a K st at beg and end of each row.

Keeping rib correct as now set, cont as folls:

**Row 2:** Rib 107 [157: 107], wrap next st (by slipping next st from left needle onto right needle, taking yarn to opposite side of work between needles and then slipping same st back onto left needle - when working back across wrapped sts work the wrapped st and the wrapping loop tog as one st) and turn.

**Row 3:** Rib 58 [94: 58], wrap next st and turn.

**Row 4:** Rib 61 [98: 61], wrap next st and turn.

**Row 5:** Rib 64 [102: 64], wrap next st and turn.

**Row 6:** Rib 67 [106: 67], wrap next st and turn.

**Row 7:** Rib 70 [110: 70], wrap next st and turn.

**Row 8:** Rib 73 [114: 73], wrap next st and turn.

**Row 9:** Rib 76 [118: 76], wrap next st and turn.

Cont in this way, working 3 [4: 3] more sts on every row before wrapping next st and turning, until the foll row has been worked:

**Row 31:** Rib 142 [206: 142], wrap next st and turn.

**Row 32 (WS of collar):** Rib to end.

Work in rib across all sts until collar meas 7 cm **from pick-up row at front neck edge**, ending with RS of collar facing for next row.

Cast off in rib.

### Sizes S-M and XXL

Join sleeve seams. Set in sleeves using the straight cast-off method.

### Size L-XL

Join sleeve seams below markers. Set in sleeves using the square set-in method.

### All sizes

See information page for finishing instructions.

# HOLLYHOCK ● ●

| | S | M | L | XL | XXL | |
|---|---|---|---|---|---|---|
| To fit bust | 81-86 | 91-97 | 102-107 | 112-117 | 122-127 | cm |
| | 32-34 | 36-38 | 40-42 | 44-46 | 48-50 | in |

**Rowan Summerlite**

| | 6 | 8 | 9 | 10 | 12 | x 50gm |
|---|---|---|---|---|---|---|

(photographed in Washed Linen 418)

## Needles

1 pair 3mm (no 11) (US 2/3) needles
2.50mm (no 12) (US B1/C2) crochet hook
6.00mm (no 4) (US J10) crochet hook

## Tension

28 sts and 36 rows to 10 cm measured over st st using 3mm (US 2/3) needles. Crochet panel is 19 cm wide, with 12 rows (2 patt repeats) measuring 22 cm using 6.00mm (US J10) crochet hook and yarn DOUBLE.

## Crochet abbreviations

**ch** = chain; **dc** = double crochet; **dtr** = double treble; **sp(s)** = space(s); **ss** = slip stitch; **tr** = treble; **yoh** = yarn over hook; **dtr2tog** = *(yoh) twice and insert hook as indicated, yoh and draw loop through, (yoh and draw through 2 loops) twice, rep from * once more, yoh and draw through all 3 loops on hook; **dtr3tog** = *(yoh) twice and insert hook as indicated,

yoh and draw loop through, (yoh and draw through 2 loops) twice; rep from * twice more, yoh and draw through all 4 loops on hook.

## BACK and FRONT (both alike)

### Crochet panel

Using 6.00mm (US J10) crochet hook and yarn DOUBLE make 22 ch.
**Foundation row (RS):** 1 tr into 3rd ch from hook, 1 tr into each of next 2 ch, 3 ch, miss 3 ch, 1 tr into each of next 7 ch, 3 ch, miss 3 ch, 1 tr into each of last 4 ch, turn.
Now work in patt as folls:
**Row 1 (WS):** 2 ch (counts as 1 tr), miss st at base of 2 ch, 1 tr between tr just missed and next tr, 1 tr between next 2 tr, 2 ch, miss 2 tr, (dtr3tog, 2 ch and dtr3tog) into next ch sp, 2 ch, miss 2 tr, 1 tr between tr just missed and next tr, (1 tr between next 2 tr) 3 times, 2 ch, miss 2 tr, (dtr3tog, 2 ch and dtr3tog) into next ch sp, 2 ch, miss 2 tr, 1 tr between tr just missed and next tr, 1 tr between next 2 sts, 1 tr into top of 2 ch at beg of previous row, turn.
**Row 2:** 5 ch (counts as 1 tr and 2 ch), miss first 3 tr and next 2 ch, *dtr3tog into next dtr3tog, 2 ch, dtr3tog into next ch sp, 2 ch, dtr3tog into next dtr3tog*, 2 ch, miss (2 ch and 2 tr), 1 tr between tr just missed and next tr, 2 ch, miss (2 tr and 2 ch), rep from * to * once more, 2 ch, miss (2 ch and 2 tr), 1 tr into top of 2 ch at beg of previous row, turn.
**Row 3:** 5 ch (counts as 1 tr and 2 ch), miss tr at end of previous row and next 2 ch, *1 tr into next dtr3tog, (2 tr into next ch sp, 1 tr into next dtr3tog) twice*, 3 ch, miss (2 ch, 1 tr and 2 ch), rep from * to * once more, 2 ch, 1 tr into 3rd of 5 ch at beg of previous row, turn.
**Row 4:** 4 ch (counts as 1 tr and 1 ch), miss tr at base of 4 ch, dtr3tog into first ch sp, *2 ch, miss 2 tr, 1 tr between tr just missed and next tr, (1 tr between next 2 tr) 3 times, 2 ch, miss 2 tr*, (dtr3tog, 2 ch and dtr3tog) into next ch sp, rep from * to * once more, dtr3tog into last ch sp, 1 ch, 1 tr into 3rd of 5 ch at beg of previous row, turn.
**Row 5:** 4 ch (does NOT count as st), 1 dtr into first ch sp, 2 ch, dtr3tog into next dtr3tog, *2 ch, miss (2 ch and 2 tr), 1 tr between tr just missed

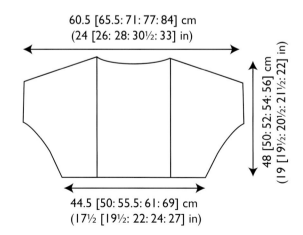

60.5 [65.5: 71: 77: 84] cm
(24 [26: 28: 30½: 33] in)

48 [50: 52: 54: 56] cm
(19 [19½: 20½: 21½: 22] in)

44.5 [50: 55.5: 61: 69] cm
(17½ [19½: 22: 24: 27] in)

and next tr, 2 ch, miss (2 tr and 2 ch)*, dtr3tog into next dtr3tog, 2 ch, dtr3tog into next ch sp, 2 ch, dtr3tog into next dtr3tog, rep from * to * once more, dtr3tog into next dtr3tog, 2 ch, dtr**2**tog into 3rd of 4 ch at beg of previous row, turn.

**Row 6**: 2 ch (counts as 1 tr), miss st at base of 2 ch, 2 tr into first ch sp, 1 tr into next dtr3tog, *3 ch, miss (2 ch, 1 tr and 2 ch)*, 1 tr into next dtr3tog, (2 tr into next ch sp, 1 tr into next dtr3tog) twice, rep from * to * once more, 1 tr into next dtr3tog, 2 tr into next ch sp, 1 tr into next dtr and turn (remembering "4 ch" at beg of previous row does NOT count as st).

These 6 rows form patt.

Cont in patt for a further 16 rows, ending after patt row 4. (Panel should meas approx 42.5 cm.)

Fasten off.

### First side edging

With RS facing, using 2.50mm (US B1/C2) crochet hook and yarn SINGLE, attach yarn at foundation ch edge, 1 ch (does NOT count as st), now work up row-end edge of crochet panel (working around the stems of ch lengths, dtr and trs) as folls: 4 dc into first row-end edge, *2 dc into next row-end edge, 6 dc into next row-end edge, 4 dc into next row-end edge, 6 dc into next row-end edge**, 6 dc into next row-end edge, 4 dc into next row-end edge; rep from * to end, ending last rep at **, turn. 106 sts.

**Next row**: 1 ch (does NOT count as st), 1 dc into each dc to end.

Fasten off.

### Second side edging

With RS facing, using 2.50mm (US B1/C2) crochet hook and yarn SINGLE, attach yarn at end of last row of crochet panel, 1 ch (does NOT count as st), now work down second row-end edge of crochet panel (working around the stems of ch lengths, dtr and trs) as folls: 6 dc into first row-end edge, *4 dc into next row-end edge, 6 dc into next row-end edge, 2 dc into next row-end edge, 4 dc into next row-end edge**, 6 dc into next row-end edge, 6 dc into next row-end edge; rep from * to end, ending last rep at **, turn. 106 sts.

**Next row**: 1 ch (does NOT count as st), 1 dc into each dc to end.

Fasten off.

### First side section

With RS facing, using 3mm (US 2/3) needles and yarn SINGLE, pick up and knit 106 sts from top of last row of first side edging – this is one knitted st for each crochet st.

**Next row (WS)**: P4, inc in next st, (P7, inc in next st) 12 times, P5. 119 sts.

Beg with a K row, now work in st st throughout as folls:

***Inc 1 st at end of next row and at same edge on foll 7 [6: 3: 2: 0] alt rows, then on foll 0 [4: 10: 14: 18] rows, ending with **WS** facing for next row. 127 [130: 133: 136: 138] sts.

Cast on 3 [6: 9: 12: 15] sts at beg of next row, ending with RS facing for next row. 130 [136: 142: 148: 153] sts.

This completes neck shaping.

Now start to shape shoulder seam as folls:

Dec 1 st at end of 3rd [5th: 5th: 5th: 7th] and 0 [4: 6: 8: 10] foll 6th rows, then on 6 [1: 0: 0: 0] foll 4th rows. 123 [130: 135: 139: 142] sts.

Work 1 [3: 5: 1: 1] rows, ending with RS facing for next row.

Now shape side and underarm seam as folls:

Cast off 6 sts at beg of next row, 5 sts at beg of foll alt row, 4 sts at beg of foll alt row, then 3 sts at beg of foll alt row, ending with **WS** facing for next row, **and at same time** dec 1 st at shoulder edge of 3rd [next: next: 5th: 5th] and foll 4th [4th: 6th: 0: 0] row. 103 [110: 115: 120: 123] sts.

Dec 1 st at end (side seam/underarm edge) of next row and at same edge on foll 23 [29: 31: 37: 41] rows, then on foll 15 [13: 14: 11: 9] alt rows **and at same time** dec 1 st at shoulder edge of 4th [2nd: 6th: 4th: 4th] and 0 [0: 0: 2: 5: 9] foll 6th rows, then on 12 [13: 10: 6: 0] foll 4th rows. 51 [53: 56: 59: 62] sts.

Work 1 row, ending with RS facing for next row.

Cast off.

### Second side section

With RS facing, using 3mm (US 2/3) needles and yarn SINGLE, pick up and knit 106 sts from top of last row of second side edging – this is one knitted st for each crochet st.

**Next row (WS)**: P4, inc in next st, (P7, inc in next st) 12 times, P5. 119 sts.

Beg with a K row, now work in st st throughout as folls:

Work 1 row.

Now complete to match first side section from ***, reading RS for WS and vice versa.

MAKING UP

Press as described on the information page.

Join shoulder seams.

### Neck edging

With RS facing, using 2.50mm (US B1/C2) crochet hook and yarn SINGLE, attach yarn at top of left shoulder seam, 1 ch (does NOT count as st), work 1 row of dc evenly around entire neck edge, working a multiple of 4 dc and ending with ss to first dc, turn.

**Next round**: 1 ch (does NOT count as st), 1 dc into each dc to end, ss to first dc, turn.

**Next round**: 1 ch (does NOT count as st), 1 dc into each of first 2 dc, *3 ch, 1 ss into 3rd ch from hook**, 1 dc into each of next 4 dc; rep from * to end, ending last rep at **, 1 dc into each of last 2 dc, ss to first dc.

Fasten off.

Join side and underarm seams.

### Cuff edgings (both alike)

Work as given for neck edging, attaching yarn at base of sleeve seam.

### Hem edging

Work as given for neck edging, attaching yarn at base of left side seam.

See information page for finishing instructions.

# D A I S Y

|  | S | M-L | XL-XXL |  |
|---|---|---|---|---|
| To fit bust | 81-86 | 91-107 | 112-127 | cm |
|  | 32-34 | 36-42 | 44-50 | in |

| Rowan Summerlite | 7 | 10 | 12 | x 50gm |
|---|---|---|---|---|

(photographed in Pure White 417)

## Crochet hook
2.50mm (no 12) (US B1/C2) crochet hook

## Tension
Based on a tension of 25 treble sts measuring 10 cm using 2.50mm (US B1/C2) crochet hook. 1 patt repeat (21 rows) measures 14 cm using 2.50mm (US B1/C2) crochet hook.

## Crochet abbreviations
**ch** = chain; **dc** = double crochet; **sp(s)** = space(s); **ss** = slip stitch; **tr** = treble; **yoh** = yarn over hook; **cluster** = (yoh and insert hook as indicated for first "leg", yoh and draw loop through loosely) twice – 5 loops on hook and first "leg" of cluster completed, (yoh and insert hook as indicated for 2nd "leg", yoh and draw loop through loosely) twice – 9 loops on hook and 2nd "leg" of cluster completed, yoh and draw through 8 loops, yoh and draw through rem 2 loops on hook; **half cluster** = (yoh and insert hook as indicated, yoh and draw loop through loosely) twice

– 5 loops on hook, yoh and draw through 4 loops, yoh and draw through rem 2 loops on hook; **tr2tog** = (yoh and insert hook as indicated, yoh and draw loop through, yoh and draw through 2 loops) twice, yoh and draw through all 3 loops on hook.

## SLEEVES
### Cuff border (worked downwards)
Using 2.50mm (US B1/C2) crochet hook, make 72 [90: 108] ch and join with a ss to form a ring.
**Foundation round (RS):** 1 ch (does NOT count as st), 1 dc into ch at base of 1 ch, *miss 2 ch, 5 tr into next ch, miss 2 ch, 1 dc into next ch; rep from * to end, replacing dc at end of last rep with ss to first dc.
Now work in border patt as folls:
**Round 1:** 3 ch (counts as 1 tr), 2 tr into dc at base of 3 ch, *miss 2 tr, 1 dc into next tr, 1 ch, miss (2 tr and 1 dc), 1 half cluster into next tr, (2 ch, 1 cluster into tr just worked into and next tr) 4 times, 2 ch, 1 half cluster into tr just worked into, 1 ch, miss (1 dc and 2 tr), 1 dc into next tr, miss 2 tr**, 5 tr into next dc; rep from * to end, ending last rep at **, 2 tr into same dc as tr at beg of round, ss to top of 3 ch at beg of round. 4 [5: 6] patt reps.
**Round 2:** 1 ch (does NOT count as st), 1 dc into st at base of 1 ch, *miss (2 tr, 1 dc and 1 ch), 1 half cluster into next st, (2 ch, 1 cluster into st just used and next st missing 2 ch in between these 2 sts) 5 times, 2 ch, 1 half cluster into st just worked into, miss (1 ch, 1 dc and 2 tr), 1 dc into next tr; rep from * to end, replacing dc at end of last rep with ss to first dc.
**Round 3:** 1 ch (does NOT count as st), 1 dc into st at base of 1 ch, *(1 dc into next st, 2 dc into next ch sp) 6 times, 1 dc into each of next 2 sts; rep from * to end, replacing last dc of last rep with ss to first dc.
**Round 4:** 1 ch (does NOT count as st), 1 dc into st at base of 1 ch, *miss 3 dc, (5 tr into next dc, miss 2 dc, 1 dc into next dc, miss 2 dc) twice, 5 tr into next dc, miss 3 dc, 1 dc into next dc; rep from * to end, replacing dc at end of last rep with ss to first dc.
These 4 rounds form border patt.
Cont in border patt for a further 7 rounds.

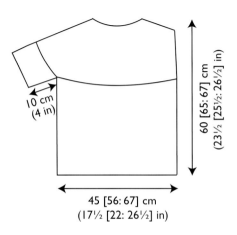

10 cm (4 in)

45 [56: 67] cm (17½ [22: 26½] in)

60 [65: 67] cm (23½ [25½: 26½] in)

66

Fasten off.
## Upper edging (worked upwards)
With RS facing and using 2.50mm (US B1/C2) crochet hook, attach yarn to foundation ch edge of cuff border at beg and end of rounds and work around foundation ch edge as folls: 3 ch (counts as 1 tr), work 69 [76: 83] tr evenly into ch sps around round (this is 3 tr into each ch sp but only 2 tr into 3 [14: 25] of these ch sps evenly spaced around), ss to top of 3 ch at beg of round, turn. 70 [77: 84] sts.
Fasten off.

## BODY (worked in one piece)
### Hem border (worked downwards)
Using 2.50mm (US B1/C2) crochet hook, make 252 [306: 378] ch and join with a ss to form a ring.
Work foundation round as given for sleeves. 14 [17: 21] patt reps. 42 [51: 63] shells.
Beg with round 1, work in border patt as given for sleeves for 11 [15: 15] rounds.
Fasten off.

### Main section (worked upwards)
With RS facing and using 2.50mm (US B1/C2) crochet hook, attach yarn to foundation ch edge of hem border at beg and end of rounds and work around foundation ch edge as folls: 3 ch (counts as 1 tr), work 223 [279: 335] tr evenly into ch sps around round (this is 3 tr into each ch sp but only 2 tr into 29 [27: 43] of these ch sps evenly spaced around), ss to top of 3 ch at beg of round, turn. 224 [280: 336] sts.
Now work in main patt as folls:
**Round 1**: 6 ch (counts as 1 tr and 3 ch), miss st at base of 6 ch and next 2 tr, *1 tr into each of next 2 tr, 3 ch, miss 2 tr; rep from * to last st, 1 tr into last st, ss to 3rd of 6 ch at beg of round. 56 [70: 84] ch sps.
**Round 2**: Ss across and into centre of first ch sp, 3 ch (counts as 1 tr), 4 tr into same ch sp, 5 tr into each ch sp to end, ss to top of 3 ch at beg of round.
**Round 3**: 1 ch (does NOT count as st), miss st at base of 1 ch, ss into each of next 2 tr, 3 ch (counts as 1 tr), 1 tr into next tr, 2 ch, miss 3 tr, *1 tr into each of next 2 tr, 2 ch, miss 3 tr; rep from * to end, ending with ss to top of 3 ch at beg of round.
**Round 4**: 3 ch (counts as 1 tr), miss st at base of 3 ch, 1 tr into next tr, *2 tr into next ch sp**, 1 tr into each of next 2 tr; rep from * to end, ending last rep at **, ss to top of 3 ch at beg of round.
**Round 5**: 3 ch (counts as 1 tr), miss st at base of 3 ch, 1 tr into each tr to end, ss to top of 3 ch at beg of round.
**Round 6**: 1 ch (does NOT count as st), (2 dc into st at base of 1 ch) 1 [0: 0] times, (miss st at base of 1 ch) 0 [1: 0] times, (1 dc into st at base of 1 ch) 0 [0: 1] times, 1 dc into each of next 0 [2: 1] tr, *4 ch, ss to 4th ch from hook**, 1 dc into each of next 3 tr; rep from * to end, ending last rep at **, 1 dc into last dc, ss to first dc. 75 [93: 112] patt reps.
**Round 7**: 5 ch (counts as 1 tr and 2 ch), miss (st at base of 5 ch, 1 dc, 4 ch, 1 ss and 1 dc), *1 tr into next dc, 2 ch, miss (1 dc, 4 ch, 1 ss and 1 dc); rep from * to end, ss to 3rd of 5 ch at beg of round.
**Round 8**: 1 ch (does NOT count as st), 1 dc into st at base of 1 ch, *(1 dc, 4 ch, ss to 4th ch from hook, 1 dc) into next ch sp, 1 dc into next tr;

rep from * to end, replacing dc at end of last rep with ss to first dc.
**Rounds 9 and 10**: As rounds 7 and 8.
**Round 11**: As round 7.
**Round 12**: 3 ch (counts as 1 tr), miss st at base of 3 ch, 1 [3: 2] tr into first ch sp, 1 tr into next tr, *2 tr into next ch sp, 1 tr into next tr, rep from * to end, replacing tr at end of last rep with ss to top of 3 ch at beg of round. 224 [280: 336] sts.
**Round 13**: As round 5.
**Round 14**: 3 ch (counts as 1 tr), 3 tr into st at base of 3 ch, *miss 2 tr, 1 dc into next tr, miss 3 tr**, 7 tr into next tr; rep from * to end, ending last rep at **, 3 tr into same st as 3 tr at beg of round, ss to top of 3 ch at beg of round. 32 [40: 48] patt reps.
**Round 15**: 1 ch (does NOT count as st), 1 dc into st at base of 1 ch, *3 ch, miss 3 tr, 1 tr into next dc, 3 ch, miss 3 tr, 1 dc into next tr; rep from * to end, replacing dc at end of last rep with ss to first dc.
**Round 16**: 1 ch (does NOT count as st), 1 dc into st at base of 1 ch, *3 ch, miss 3 ch, 1 dc into next st; rep from * to end, replacing dc at end of last rep with ss to first dc.
**Round 17**: As round 16.
**Round 18**: 1 ch (does NOT count as st), 1 dc into st at base of 1 ch, *miss 3 ch, 7 tr into next dc, miss 3 ch, 1 dc into next dc; rep from * to end, replacing dc at end of last rep with ss to first dc.
**Round 19**: 5 ch (counts as 1 tr and 2 ch), miss st at base of 5 ch and next 3 tr, *1 dc into next tr, 2 ch, miss 3 tr**, 1 tr into next dc, 2 ch, miss 3 tr; rep from * to end, ending last rep at **, ss to 3rd of 5 ch at beg of round.
**Round 20**: 3 ch (counts as 1 tr), miss st at base of 3 ch, *2 tr into next ch sp, 2 tr into next dc, 2 tr into next ch sp, 1 tr into next tr; rep from * to end, replacing tr at end of last rep with ss to top of 3 ch at beg of round. 224 [280: 336] sts.
**Round 21**: As round 5.
These 21 rounds form main patt.
Work in main patt for a further 12 rounds, ending after patt round 12. (Work should meas approx 21 cm from top of hem border.)
### Shape for yoke
**Next round**: 3 ch (counts as 1 tr), miss st at base of 3 ch, 1 tr into each of next 55 [69: 83] tr, now attach first sleeve to body by working into sts of last round of sleeve, beg and ending at beg and end of sleeve rounds, by working 1 tr into each of next 70 [77: 84] sts, 1 tr into each of next 112 [140: 168] tr of body, attach second sleeve to body by working into sts of last round of this sleeve, beg and ending at beg and end of sleeve rounds, by working 1 tr into each of next 70 [77: 84] sts, 1 tr into each of last 56 [70: 84] tr of body, ss to top of 3 ch at beg of round. 364 [434: 504] sts.
Work main patt rounds 14 to 20.
**Next round**: 3 ch (counts as 1 tr), miss tr at base of 3 ch, 1 tr into each of next 16 [2: 2] tr, (tr2tog over next 2 tr, 1 tr into each of next 5 tr) 47 [61: 71] times, tr2tog over next 2 tr, 1 tr into each of last 16 [2: 2] tr, ss to top of 3 ch at beg of round. 316 [372: 432] sts.
Work main patt rounds 1 to 4.
**Next round**: 3 ch (counts as 1 tr), miss tr at base of 3 ch, 1 tr into each of next 12 [7: 1] tr, (tr2tog over next 2 tr, 1 tr into each of next 4 tr) 48 [59: 71] times, tr2tog over next 2 tr, 1 tr into each of last 13 [8: 2] tr, ss to top of 3 ch at beg of round. 267 [312: 360] sts.

**Next round:** 1 ch (does NOT count as st), 1 dc into st at base of 1 ch, 1 dc into next tr, *4 ch, ss to 4th ch from hook**, 1 dc into each of next 3 tr, rep from * to end, ending last rep at **, 1 dc into last tr, ss to first dc. 89 [104: 120] patt reps.

Work main patt rounds 7 to 12.

**Next round:** 3 ch (counts as 1 tr), miss tr at base of 3 ch, 1 tr into each of next 9 [7: 16] tr, (tr2tog over next 2 tr, 1 tr into each of next 3 tr) 49 [59: 65] times, tr2tog over next 2 tr, 1 tr into each of last 10 [7: 16] tr, ss to top of 3 ch at beg of round. 217 [252: 294] sts.

Work main patt rounds 14 to 20.

**Next round:** 3 ch (counts as 1 tr), miss tr at base of 3 ch, 1 tr into each of next 11 [6: 7] tr, (tr2tog over next 2 tr, 1 tr into each of next 2 tr) 48 [59: 69] times, tr2tog over next 2 tr, 1 tr into each of last 11 [7: 8] tr, ss to top of 3 ch at beg of round. 168 [192: 224] sts.

Work main patt rounds 1 to 4.

**Next round:** 3 ch (counts as 1 tr), miss tr at base of 3 ch, 1 tr into each of next 21 [6: 1] tr, (tr2tog over next 2 tr, 1 tr into next tr) 41 [59: 73] times, tr2tog over next 2 tr, 1 tr into each of last 21 [6: 1] tr, ss to top of 3 ch at beg of round. 126 [132: 150] sts.

**Sizes M-L and XL-XXL only**

**Next round:** 1 ch (does NOT count as st), 1 dc into st at base of 1 ch, 1 dc into next dc, *4 ch, ss to 4th ch from hook**, 1 dc into each of next 3 dc, rep from * to end, ending last rep at **, 1 dc into last dc, ss to first

dc. - [44: 50] patt reps.

Work main patt rounds 7 to – [9: 11].

**Size M-L only**

**Next round:** 3 ch (counts as 1 tr), miss st at base of 3 ch, *2 tr into next ch sp, 1 tr into next tr; rep from * to end, replacing tr at end of last rep with ss to top of 3 ch at beg of round. 132 sts.

**Size XL-XXL only**

**Next round:** 3 ch (counts as 1 tr), miss st at base of 3 ch, *(2 tr into next ch sp, 1 tr into next tr) 3 times, tr2tog into next ch sp, 1 tr into next tr; rep from * to last 2 ch sps, 2 tr into next ch sp, 1 tr into next tr, 2 tr into last ch sp, ss to top of 3 ch at beg of round. 138 sts.

**All sizes**

**Next round:** 1 ch (does NOT count as st), 1 dc into st at base of 1 ch, 1 dc into each st to end, ss to first dc, turn. 126 [132: 138] sts.

**Next round:** 1 ch (does NOT count as st), 1 dc into dc at base of 1 ch, *miss 2 dc, 5 tr into next dc, miss 2 dc, 1 dc into next dc, rep from * to end, replacing dc at end of last rep with ss to first dc.

Fasten off.

MAKING UP

Press as described on the information page.

See information page for finishing instructions.

## TENSION

Achieving the correct tension is one of the most important factors when knitting one of my designs. I cannot stress highly enough that you really do need to crochet/knit a tension square BEFORE you start to make the garment. The tension stated on each of my patterns must be achieved to ensure that the garment fits correctly and that it matches the measurements stated on the size diagram. I recommend that you crochet/knit a square using the number of stitches and rows stated on the pattern tension plus 3 or 4 stitches and rows. To check your tension, place the square on a flat surface and mark out a 10cm square using pins as markers. Count the number of stitches and rows between the pins. If you have too many stitches, then your crochet/knitting is too tight, make another square using a thicker hook/needle. If you have too few stitches, then your crochet/knitting is too loose, make another square using a thinner hook/needle. It is also important to keep checking your tension whilst you are making your garment especially if you are returning to crochet/knit after leaving your work for a period of time.

## SIZING

The patterns are written giving the instructions for the smallest size, for the other sizes work the figures in the brackets. The measurements stated on the size diagrams are the measurements of your finished garment AFTER pressing.

## MODEL SIZE

Georgia is 5' 8'' tall and is a standard size 8/10 and she is wearing the smallest size in each photograph.

## FINISHING

Finishing your garment beautifully is another important factor when making one of my designs. Good finishing will ensure that your garment fits correctly and washes and wears well. I urge you to spend time pressing and stitching your garment together, after all you've just spent a lot money and time knitting it using lovely Rowan yarns and the last thing you want to do is ruin it with bad finishing!

## PRESSING

Firstly sew in any loose ends to the wrong side of the work. Block out each piece and then press according to the care instructions stated on the yarn ball bands. Always press using an iron on the wrong side of the work over a protective cloth (this can be damp or dry) and have the steam setting switched on the iron. Pay particular attention to the sides or edges of each piece as this will make the sewing up both easier and neater. Take special care with the welts and cuffs of the design – if the garment is fitted then gently steam the ribs so that they fill out but remain elastic. If the garment is a boxy, straight shape then steam press out the ribs to correct width.

## STITCHING

When stitching the pieces together, remember to match areas of texture or pattern very carefully where they meet. I recommend that you use mattress stitch wherever possible, this stitch gives the neatest finish ensuring that the seam lays flat.

Having crocheted/knitted your pieces according to the pattern instructions, generally the shoulder seams of the front and back are now joined together using mattress stitch. Work the neck trim according to the pattern instructions and then join the neckband seams using mattress stitch if required. Crochet/knit neck bands or collars to the length stated in the pattern instructions, slightly stretching the trims before measuring. Please take extra care when stitching the edgings and collars around the neck of the garment as these control the stretch of the neck. The sleeves are now normally added to the garment, take care to match the centre of the sleeve head to the shoulder seam. Ideally stretch the sleeve head into the armhole and stitch in place, if the sleeve head is too large for the armhole then check your tension as your crochet/knitting may be too loose. Join the underarm and side seams. Slip stitch any pockets or pocket lining into place and sew on buttons corresponding to the button holes lining up the outside edge of the button with the edging join or seam.

Carefully press your finished garment again to the measurements stated on the size diagram.

## AFTERCARE

Ensure that you wash and dry your garment according to the care instructions stated on the yarn ball bands. If your garment uses more than one type of yarn then wash according to the most delicate. Reshape your garment when slightly damp and then carefully press to size again.

## BUTTONS

The buttons used on the garments in this collection were from various sources. I recommend that you contact Bedecked Haberdashery to find similar buttons:

Bedecked Haberdashery,
Barningham Park Coach House
Barningham, Nr RICHMOND
North Yorkshire
DL11 7DW
United Kingdom
Tel: +44 (0)1833 621 451
Email: thegirls@bedecked.co.uk

## EXPERIENCE RATING

For guidance only.

⬤ suitable for a beginner crocheter/knitter with a little experience.

⬤ ⬤ suitable for a crocheter/knitter with average ability.

⬤ ⬤ ⬤ suitable for the experienced crocheter/knitter.

## CROCHET ABBREVIATIONS

The crochet patterns are written in the English style, however I am aware that the terminology varies from country to country. To help you, listed below are the English abbreviations with the US alternatives.

| ENGLISH | | US | |
|---|---|---|---|
| ch | chain | ch | chain |
| dc | double crochet | sc | single crochet |
| htr | half treble | hdc | half double crochet |
| tr | treble | dc | double crochet |
| dtr | double treble | tr | treble |

## KNITTING ABBREVIATIONS

| K | knit |
|---|---|
| P | purl |
| st(s) | stitch(es) |
| inc | increas(e)(ing) |
| dec | decreas(e)(ing) |
| st st | stocking stitch (1 row K, 1 row P) |
| g st | garter stitch (K every row) |
| beg | begin(ning) |
| foll | following |
| rem | remain(ing) |
| rev st st | reverse stocking stitch (1 row K, 1 row P) |
| rep | repeat |
| alt | alternate |
| cont | continue |
| patt | pattern |
| tog | together |
| mm | millimetres |
| cm | centimetres |
| in(s) | inch(es) |
| RS | right side |
| WS | wrong side |
| sl 1 | slip one stitch |
| psso | pass slip stitch over |
| p2sso | pass 2 slipped stitches over |
| tbl | through back of loop |
| M1 | make one stitch by picking up the horizontal loop before the next stitch and knitting into the back of it |
| M1P | make one stitch by picking up the horizontal loop before the next stitch and purling into the back of it |
| yfwd | yarn forward |
| yrn | yarn round needle |
| meas | measures |
| 0 | no stitches, times or rows |
| - | no stitches, times or rows for that size |
| yon | yarn over needle |
| yfrn | yarn forward round needle |
| wyib | with yarn at back |

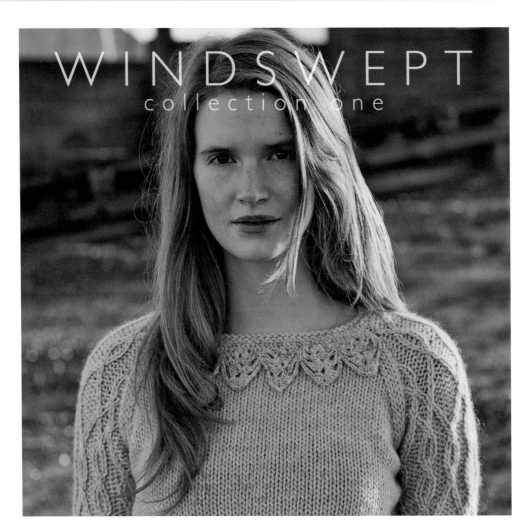

WINDSWEPT
collection one

12 handknit designs for women by Marie Wallin

Printed book available from Rowan stockists.
Pattern downloads will be available soon from **www.mariewallin.com**

14 handknit designs for women and the home by Marie Wallin

Printed book available from **www.mariewallin.com** and Rowan stockists.